CHRISTIANITY

AND

THE NEW AGE RELIGION

A BRIDGE TOWARD MUTUAL UNDERSTANDING

DR. L. DAVID MOORE

PENDULUM PLUS PRESS
ATLANTA, GA

PENDULUM
PLUS

Acknowledgments are presented on Page 243

First Edition, 1993

ISBN 0-9635665-0-4

Library of Congress Catalog Card Number 92-82117

Published by
PENDULUM PLUS PRESS
3232 Cobb Parkway
Suite 414
Atlanta, GA 30339

Printed in the United States of America
10 9 8 7 6 5 4 3 2 1

TABLE OF CONTENTS

CHRISTIANITY AND THE NEW AGE RELIGION

Table of Contents

NOTES FROM THE AUTHOR

The purpose for this book is addressed in the Introduction. In summary, it is to give those of the New Age some understanding of the beliefs of Christianity, and vice versa. I feel this book is needed, because there is a lot of misunderstanding of the purposes of each religion, and a lot of mistrust about the aims of each.

I have had and am having a wonderful life. I have degrees from three major universities and certificates from three others. The degrees include a Ph. D. in Chemistry from Purdue University; and the certificates include advanced management training at the University of Chicago and at Harvard. I have been in the top officer echelon of major corporations and have been President of what was described in a national magazine as ''the fastest growing, most exciting specialty chemical company in the United States.'' I was raised in a Christian home, and have taught Adult Sunday School for over 20 years, the last six in the largest Presbyterian Church in the U. S. I have been married for over 36 years to the same wonderful woman. We have four children and two grandchildren, all of whom I love very much. I want all of them to understand themselves, their world and their religion.

I go into this background to indicate that in my mind, I am no kook or cultist. I have thought deeply and seriously about religion and the meaning of life. I have thoroughly investigated the entire realm of the practice of Christianity, and have accepted some aspects and rejected others just as every Christian has whether he admits it or not. I have investigated much of the realm of religious practice generally known as the New Age, and have accepted some aspects and rejected others just as every New Ager has whether he admits it or not. Within those New Age aspects which I have accepted, I have found love and support without judgment and guilt. I truly wish I could say the same about all parts of the religion into which I was born, for I believe that was the original intent of Christianity. I feel the need to write this book so that the religion into which I was born and which I still practice, could understand that there is something meaningful in the new religion which should not be ignored.

This book is not a spy novel or any other type of escape reading. Instead, it is intended to create understanding. The book starts very slowly, for that is the only way to make progress without confusing or losing anyone. However, each Chapter is written as an independent Chapter. If the reader wants to move slowly and with understanding, then he should start at the beginning and go at whatever pace feels comfortable. If, on the other hand, the reader wants to start out with some elements of ''Gee Whiz'', then Chapters 5 or 6 would be appropriate; or if he wants some controversy, then Chapter 7 will do nicely. But in either case, to understand the ''why'' of what is presented and maybe to accept it, the reader would then have to go back to the beginning and proceed slowly.

The New Ager will find little of a ''Gee Whiz'' nature in the material of this book for that is not its purpose. Nevertheless, he may gain some understanding as to why the ''Gee Whiz'' material that he has encountered in other books is so logical or rational.

The term "New Age" is objected to by many in the movement. However, as mentioned in the Introduction, it is a name which communicates. As such, it will be used until something more appropriate or descriptive is developed.

In this book, I have used the words "he", "him", "himself" and the like. I mean them to designate a human; I do not mean them to designate a particular sex. I know that some are offended by these terms because they consider them to represent the belief that females are in some way less than males. I do not believe that they are; and in fact, I find myself racing to catch up with some of the concepts presented by the females I know. I will admit that I tried writing this book with "he/she", or "him/her", or "herself/himself", or even with "hum" as an attempt to stand for a human being of either sex, but I found that I could not follow the intended sentence structure or in any other way make sense out of what I was trying to write. And so, for those to whom it is important, I apologize. The use of the masculine pronouns to stand for either sex was the way I was taught to write, and an "old dog" may have difficulty learning new tricks. I do not in any way intend to imply inferiority. That is as far from my true belief as it is possible to get.

I have written and had published two books prior to this one. They are on economics and were published under a "nom de plume". This is the first book to which I will put my real name and let the chips fall where they may!

Important notes: As a concerned author, I feel that I again have to emphasize that this is not an escape novel or a book to be read in any sort of light-hearted manner. Instead, it is a book which was written to transmit understanding. I have had many friends who have read early drafts of this book. Without exception they

11

told me that they would go rolling merrily along, agreeing with everything that had been said and averaging a page a minute when all of a sudden, they would get stopped by a page that dug deeply into their psyche. They then spent an hour or more on that single page. One person told me that he returned to one page several times and wrestled with it until he came to a conclusion that he could accept within his innermost being. And the unusual part is that no two people have been struck with the same page. Seemingly, there is something in here for almost everyone, and that something differs from person to person. The two sections which have caused almost universal comment have been the last two sections: **Chapter 9 Conclusion** and the **Epilogue.** As an author, I hope that the readers' preference for these two efforts was because the book was nearing its end, and not because the prior material was less worthy.

In addition, I feel I must say that this book was written with the belief that an individual can believe in Jesus Christ and accept him as the one to be followed without having to accept concepts which have been introduced by man. Concepts such as ''the only son of God''; and ''born of a virgin''; and ''the Trinity''; and ''eternal damnation'' are **not** contained in the scriptures as written in their original language. And they were never promulgated by Jesus the Christ.

Finally, I feel obliged to say that there is much more that can be written on the interaction between Christianity and the New Age religion. In particular, the statements made by some of the early Fathers of the Church [St. Clement the Great, St. Jerome, St. Augustine and St. Francis among others] bear a remarkable similarity to statements being made by some of the New Age participants of today. That comparison should be pulled together. If there is any desire on the part of the readers of this book to hear more on this subject, I will be happy to oblige. In the meantime, I hope that this book can serve as the first step across the bridge toward mutual understanding between fellow believers.

INTRODUCTION

Since man first came to believe that there was a ''something'' which was more than he, man has followed his religion. The word ''religion'' is derived from the Latin *religio* which means ''bond between man and the gods'', and which, in turn, comes from two Latin words: *ligare* meaning ''to bind'' and *re* meaning ''back''. Consequently, when man follows his religion, he is following the path which will ''bind him back to God''.

Man is far from being a perfect creature. One of his imperfections is related to fighting for his beliefs with the attitude that no other belief is possible. This ''I am right and you are wrong'' attitude has led to many activities in support of his belief. Some of those activities have generated positive results such as the passive attitudes expressed by Thomas a' Becket, Thomas More and many others who would not let their belief be swayed by others, but who also would not harm others in an attempt to impose their beliefs on them. Other activities have generated negative results such as the Crusades, the Inquisition, the Plunder of the native wealth and heritage of all the Americas in the name of the European Christ, the Salem Witch Trials, and many others during which the believer attempted to impose his beliefs on others by means of war, force, torture, character assassination or the like.

Christians have had a long and sorry history of using force to impose their belief on others, a history which is almost as sorry as that of Islam. Many Christians have abhorred such acts, for they are acts which have been done in an attempt to control others. It is probable that some Christians have felt obliged to act this way because of what they understood the Great Commission to be. That commissioning of Christian disciples is presented in Matthews 28: 18-20 and says, ''And Jesus came and said to them, 'All authority in heaven and on earth has been given to me. Go therefore and make disciples of all nations, baptizing them in the name of the Father and of the Son and of the Holy Spirit, teaching them to observe all that I have commanded you; and lo, I am with you always, to the close of the age' ''. Some Christians have attempted to fulfill that commission whatever it took, possibly in the belief that the end justified the means. A few such examples are mentioned above.

In addition to physical force, another activity has been developed to support the Faith. That activity is a branch of Christian theology known as ''Apologetics''. Apologetics is considered to be the intellectual defense of the truth of Christianity. It is traditionally positive in its direct argument for Christianity and negative in its criticism of opposing beliefs. Apologetics often has a difficult time in not becoming dogmatic by refusing to take seriously the objections of non-Christians. In addition, Apologetics has a difficult time not becoming replaced by Polemics which is the defense of the beliefs of a particular sect of Christianity against the beliefs of other Christian sects.[1] Polemics also has a difficult time not becoming dogmatic by having a closed mind, one example of which is presented by the frequent the use of the coined phrase, ''Biblical Christian'', a Polemic phrase which is intended to imply that other Christians do not accept the Bible as their authority.

With the exception of the Christian Apologetics against the

Greco-Roman culture in the first and second century AD which stopped when Christianity became the state religion, Apologetics has not been practiced until the past two hundred years or so. In fact, until the eighteenth century, Christianity showed little inclination to study non-Christian religions. As a few examples, when Manichaeism was developed in the fourth century AD, the Christian church ignored it rather than feeling the need to defend itself, since this "new religion" was merely considered to be a Christian heresy. In addition, when Islam was founded in the seventh century, the Christian church not only ignored it by considering it to be Christian heresy rather than a new religion, it went so far as to forbid translation of the Koran and, in fact, jailed the theologian who published a translation in 1543 and then ordered that his book be burned. Finally, Christianity effectively ignored Buddhism until almost the nineteenth century. In Christian writings, Buddhism was mentioned once in AD 200, then was absent for the next 1300 years. This habit of neglecting anything not Christian was probably based on two attitudes inherited from Judaism; [1] that the pagan gods are "nothing" when compared to the true God, the Creator of the world; and [2] that all pagan gods are demonic forces engaged in mortal combat with the true God. The second item is particularly important to Christians who define the history of salvation as concluding with a final struggle between Christ with his church on one side, and the Antichrist with his thrones on the other. The final victory will belong to Christ.[2]

With the publication of the Apology of the Augsburg Confession in 1531 which defended the Lutheran Faith against the Roman Catholic Faith, Polemics became actively practiced. This was followed by the polemic activities of other reformed Christian church movements. With such good practice in internecine warfare within the Christian church, it was only natural that Apologetics would start to be practiced against other religions in an attempt to win over man's soul, worldwide. Consequently, Apologetics fought Deism in the eighteenth century, sponsored the great missionary movement of the nineteenth century, and has fought the materialistic ideologies of the twentieth century.

And thus, Apologetics or "the intellectual defense of the Faith" has progressed from a defense against Hellenistic culture, to a "stick your head in the sand and ignore them" approach against other religions, to an internecine warfare against itself which continues today, and finally to a recognition that other religions exist against which intellectual warfare must be fought.

Today, the Christian Apologists have found a new challenge. It is known by most people as the New Age Religion. Although many in the movement do not like that name, it will be used in this book as a communicative tool. The name will suffice until another is developed and generally accepted. Against this New Age religion, Apologetics is being applied in full force, principally by the "Biblical Christians". In response to the New Age challenge, the Apologists are stating that all New Age practices reside in cults, each of which is lead by a human who believes himself to be God's exclusive messenger to the world, each of which is self-centered rather than God-centered, and most of which make false prophecies, practice Pantheism and/or practice mantra meditation which, of course, is the practice of Hinduism. In addition, all self-centered cult leaders make a lot of money. On the other hand, many New Age Apologists have assumed that Christianity is their challenge and thus have rejected anything related to the Judeo-Christian God or to Jesus Christ. In between these two camps are the majority of the New Agers. They are sincere people who are not members of a cult, but who believe that many aspects of the New Age Religious movement not only make sense, they expand Christianity. These people might be found in the established churches on Sunday and possibly at Tuesday or Wednesday Bible Study searching the Bible for truth as they can understand it, while spending some other portions of the week studying the writings on Edgar Cayce, or The Keys of Enoch, or the I AM literature, or The Aquarian Gospel of Jesus Christ for truth as they can understand it. And they would be found doing both with an open mind. These people abhor the abuses of some New Age practitioners, just as they abhor the abuses done by some in the name of Christ, particularly when either has been done in an attempt to control others; but in neither case do they let the good be thrown away with the bad. These people are sincere in their beliefs. They may well represent the fastest, or at least one of the fastest growing religious movements in the country today.

For those in the more established religions, it might help if an open mind could be maintained which would allow an investigation of the New Age Religion on an acceptance-rejection basis, instead of categorically rejecting that which is not understood. The acceptance-rejection basis might have several steps such as: [1] to accept that which fits within God's will and is positive for the individual; [2] to reject that which is not; [3] to resist forcing one's opinion upon another or trying to control the free-will choices of another; and [4] not to judge the actions of another so long as those actions are not harmful to a third person. Possibly this book could help to instigate such an acceptance-rejection procedure.

In that light, the purpose of this book is to address Christianity and the New Age Religion, including their similarities, their differences, their misunderstandings and whether a discontinuity or continuum exists between any parts of them. The major purpose of this book is to provide some Christian teaching for the New Age practitioners who reject Christianity, so that they might start to see that the positive growth made over the past two thousand years is not to be rejected out-of-hand; while also providing enough New Age insight to the Christian practitioners so that they might see that there is something positive in New Age which can be accepted without destroying their Christianity. It is not the intent of this book to preach one belief over another or to propose that any one belief is superior to another; instead it is an attempt to present Facts, Opinions or Beliefs and then to let the reader make his own free-will choice. It is an attempt to create a new bridge between Christianity-New Age which is similar in function, if not in erudition, to the bridge which the Letter to the Hebrews in the New Testament of the holy Bible created between Judaism-Christianity.

One of the piers in that new bridge is the concept that as religions mature, they tend to become hardened in their practice. At this point, there needs to be an introduction of a new order of things. As an example, some 2,000 years after Abraham became its Father, Judaism became strangled by the laws and the doctrines of the established religious sects such as the Pharisees and the Sadducees. Jesus Christ introduced a new order of things--**love** instead of **law.** But during the subsequent 2,000 years, the Christian Church developed its own system of doctrines, and some of them have been almost as inhibiting as the laws of the Pharisees.

Throughout all of this experience, particularly the experience of one religion's intolerance against another, religious freedom has managed to take about three steps forward for each two steps in retreat. Thus, there has been a continuing march toward religious freedom throughout this period of history. Hopefully, the following insert, the chart entitled <u>History's Continuing March Toward Religious Freedom</u> will generate some understanding about the progress made during that march; and about some of the religious intolerance which has held back the progress during that march.

HISTORY'S CONTINUING MARCH

BC

2000	
2000*	Abraham receives the covenant from God
1800*	Stonehenge is established in Britain
1700*	Jews emigrate to Egypt
1600*	"Book of the Dead", collection of religious principles, written in Egypt
1500	
1385	Ikhnaton attempts monotheism in Egypt, later overthrown
1200*	Moses receives the Ten Commandments from God
1000 1000*	David and Solomon are kings of the combined kingdoms, Israel and Judea
800*	Time of the earliest Jewish prophets [e.g. Elijah]
721*	The Northern Kingdom [Israel] is conquered and 11 of the 12 tribes are lost
701*	The death of Isaiah, the "prophet in Jerusalem"
630	Zoroaster born in Persia
586	Judea is conquered and Judaism has no nation for 2,534 years
551	Confucius born in China
500 521	Buddha becomes inspired in India
427	Plato born in Greece
400*	The "Five Books of Moses" [Pentateuch] receive their definitive form
250 300*	Alexandria is established as the center of Greek learning
165	The Book of Daniel is written
112*	The Pharisees and the Sadducees become important in Jerusalem
5*	Jesus is born sometime in the period of 4-8 BC
00	* means that the times are only approximately correct

AD

33*	Jesus the Christ is crucified on Golgotha
55*	Paul writes the Letter to the Corinthians, the earliest document which was accepted in the present New Testament
65*	The first gospel [Mark] is written. Flavius Josephus writes his history of the Jewish Wars
150*	Earliest known Sanskrit inscriptions in India
250 200*	Origen publishes the Old Testament in Greek
313	After the Battle of Milvian Bridge [312], Constantine issues the Edict of Milan which ends the persecution of Christians
380	Christianity is declared the state religion of Rome
500 484	The first split between the Eastern and the Western Churches
529	Justinian closes the world's largest school and library in Alexandria because they are non-Christian

TOWARD RELIGIOUS FREEDOM

540*	The doctrine of the Trinity is accepted by the Church	
570	Mohammed is born	
597	Cantebury is established in Britain. York is four years later	
610	Mohammed has his vision on Mount Hira	600
632	Buddhism becomes the state religion of Tibet	
641	The Arabs destroy the school and library in Alexandria in the name of their religion	
751	The four sects of Islam are established	750
879	The Pope [Rome] and the Patriarch [Constantinople] excommunicate each other	
993	The first canonization of saints	1000
1054	The cleavage between the Roman and Eastern Churches becomes permanent	
1074	The excommunication of all married priests was ordered	
1200*	The Apostle's Creed was accepted by the Roman Church	
1229	The Inquisition in Toulouse forbids Bible reading by laymen	1250
1302	Papal bull "Unam sanctum" says the Pope is supreme	
1492	Jew and Moors in Spain are ordered to convert, or be burned	
1501	Papal bull orders the burning of any book which questions the authority of the Church	1500
1517	Martin Luther posts his 95 theses and starts the Reformation	
1533-5	Henry VIII is excommunicated; English clergy abjure Pope	
1536	Tyndale, publisher of a Bible in English, is burned at the stake by soldiers of the Roman Church	
1611	The King James Version [authorized] of the Bible is published	
1633	Galileo is forced to abjure the theories of Copernicus	
1734	The Koran is translated by the Church, some 1100 years late	1750
1858	The Blessed Virgin first appears at Lourdes, France	
1924	Gandhi fasts for 21 days in protest of Hindu-Moslem riots	
1943	The U.S. Supreme Court rules that children cannot be forced to salute the U.S. flag if that is against their religion	
1968	Pope Paul VI presents a prohibition of artificial contraception	
1970	Paul VI declares priestly celibacy to be a fundamental principle of the Roman Catholic Church	
1971	The Church of England and the Roman Church end a 400 year dispute concerning the definition of the Eucharist	
1974	A Gallup Poll shows a significant reduction in church attendance in the U.S. among all established religions	
1976	The U.S. and Canadian Anglican Churches ordain women as priests; but the English and Roman Churches refuse	2000
1987	The Harmonic Convergence is celebrated by all who understand its importance	

PROLOGUE

Some time during the early part of the Christian era, a problem started to develop in the newest mystery religion of that day, the religion which worshiped God through His son, Jesus Christ. The problem involved Jews who wanted to be a part of the new religion, Christianity, while still holding on to all of the laws, traditions and teachings of their old religion, Judaism.

To help modify or even resolve the problem, a group of deep thinkers assembled to write a document which was first used as a sermon, and then later sent to other Christian churches as a letter. Today we know this document as The Letter To The Hebrews in the New Testament of the Holy Bible, but only God knows who the deep thinkers and authors were. For some time, scholars suggested that Paul was the major author; but this suggestion has been dismissed by most modern Biblical investigators. Many have suggested a Greek named Apollos as the most probable author; and some have suggested Barnabus. But the fact is that although some Biblical scholars may have ideas about who authored the Book of Hebrews, no one really knows who the author was. In fact, Origen, who has been called the greatest Christian teacher with the possible exception of the Apostles, stated in the second century AD that ''only God knows who

19

wrote Hebrews''.

However, there are things which all Biblical scholars do know about Hebrews. For example, they know that the style and content of Hebrews are different than that which was used in any of the other letters in the New Testament. The style of Hebrews is argumentative and the content is directed to all people rather than to the needs of a particular congregation or a particular person. This difference from the other letters is unusual. Next, they know that the major purpose for Hebrews has universal appeal and meaning which can extend beyond its original purpose. The original purpose for Hebrews was to develop a healing process in order to mend the growing rift between Christians and Jews; but that healing process can be extended to mend rifts between other people of good faith. This ability to extend the letter's purpose is also unusual. Finally, they know that there are mysteries in Hebrews which are not completely explained. These mysteries are of the type described in Colossians 1:26 as being ''hidden for ages and generations but now made manifest to his saints''. The majestic figure of Melchizedek is certainly one such mystery; and calling Isaac an ''only son'' in Hebrews 11:17 may be another. Such mysteries are unusual among the New Testament letters.

Hebrews was vitally needed, for at the time of its writing many Jews wanted to adopt Christianity while keeping their Judaism *in toto*. Hebrews was written primarily as a well-structured dissertation defining Christianity as the perfect religion which permits an individual to have free and unrestricted access to his God. In addition, Hebrews was written to suggest that to keep a firm hold on an imperfect religion such as Judaism would dilute the follower's ability to understand the full meaning of Christianity. Finally, Hebrews was written in an attempt to tie the two religions together in a way that would provide a bridge between the old religion and the new; or in our present thinking as a bridge between the Old Testament and the New. It did this by comparing and evaluating the pros and cons of each religion. In this way, Hebrews was meant to suggest that although people should give up their old religion in favor of the new, there really was not a complete break between the two; and, in fact, that the two constitute a continuance from the old to the new: from ancient Judaism into modern Christianity. One of the major lessons contained in Hebrews is that the good of the one need not be discarded when accepting the advances of the other. This is a universal lesson.

From the beginning, Christianity found a welcome place in the hearts of many people because it proposed an intimate relationship between the individual and his God. Although at that time many people professed a belief in God, Judaism had become a religion of Law and not of a personal relationship with God. In fact, the largest religious sect of the day, the Pharisees, had become so devoted to the Law that they had, in essence, started to worship the Law rather than God; and their worship of the Law went so far as to convert the understanding and the acceptance of the Law into a practice of worshiping the absolute letter of the Law. This changed adoring worship into ritualistic ceremony. As a consequence of this doctrinal approach, many people left the established religion in the Temple and joined new age religious sects such as the Essenes. For those who stayed in the established religion with its absence of a sense of God's love, despair crept in and caused many to believe that the world would soon come to an end.

Christianity grew at the expense of Judaism. However, Judaism survived the coming of Christianity and as a result, Judaism without Christianity is a viable religion for many today, just as Christianity without Judaism satisfies many others. But those Christians who accepted the lessons taught in Hebrews developed a more complete understanding of their Christianity than they could otherwise have developed. They became a part of the Judeo-Christian heritage, understanding the lessons of each because of their acceptance of the continuance of the old leading into the new.

Two thousand years after the birth of Christianity, a picture similar to that which occurred at the birth of Christianity is developing. At that time, many people professed a belief in God, but found dissatisfaction in His worship at the Temple. Today, although more people profess to a belief in Jesus Christ than at any other time in recorded history, membership in the established Christian churches is declining year after year. In addition, new religious sects are being developed outside the established church, and many people who stay within the established churches are expressing the belief that the world as we know it will come to an end in the near future. Finally, in a manner similar to that of the Pharisees, many established churches have become so doctrinaire that they are preaching the absolute letter of the Gospel rather than its meaning. Just as the similar circumstances of two thousand years ago provided fertile ground for the growth of Christianity outside of the established Temple, the circumstances of today are providing fertile ground for the growth of new religious sects outside the established churches.

Although the new religion being accepted by many goes by a multitude of names, in general it has been identified under the heading of New Age Religion. The parallels between the advent of Christianity during the time of Judaism and the advent of New Age Religion during the time of Christianity are striking. And just as Judaism survives today without an overlay of Christianity and Christianity survives in the complete absence of Judaism, a similar relationship will be developed between Christianity and New Age. However, just as Christianity becomes more meaningful within the continuance of the Judeo-Christian heritage as bridged by Hebrews, so will New Age become a more meaningful religion within the continuance of the Christianity-New Age heritage. As Hebrews teaches us, the good of the old need not be discarded when accepting the advances of the new.

CHAPTER 1 COMPARISON OF CHRISTIANITY AND THE NEW AGE RELIGION -- SIMILARITIES, DIFFERENCES AND MISUNDERSTANDINGS

If anyone were to take the time to investigate the religions of Christianity and New Age, they would find many similarities, some differences, and a lot of misunderstandings. The purpose of this chapter is to list and to give a short description of the similarities, differences and misunderstandings, and to refer to later chapters which will go into greater detail on many of the same subjects.

SIMILARITIES

GOD As a major point, both religions believe in the existence of a supreme being who created all that is and who reigns on high. As one minor difference, most Christians tend to refer to this entity as God, the Lord, or sometimes the Trinity; whereas

23

many New Agers tend to use God, or Mother-Father God, or YodHeyVodHey, or I AM, or the Light, or the Spiritual Being, or the Source, all of which have some historical validity. However, some New Agers object to using any name for God which has previously been used. They therefore develop names which have little or no accepted historical basis such as Creative Energy, Universal Mind and the like. As another slight difference, Christianity tends to leave the overall functioning of the cosmos to God; whereas New Age tends to have a very structured universe in which every entity has an integrated part. But these minor differences in name or function pale when compared to the major similarity: *viz.* that each religion believes in one Entity who ultimately is the creator of all things. This subject is discussed in greater detail in Chapter 2.

JESUS CHRIST Both religions believe in the existence, the divinity, and the eternality of Christ or of a Christ consciousness that is a part of the Creator God. However, there are some differences in the extent of this belief. Some of these differences are listed below in this chapter, and all are discussed in greater detail in parts of Chapter 2 and Chapter 7, and in all of Chapter 3.

SACRAMENTS Both religions believe in sacraments which have been instituted as a testament to inner grace or as a channel which mediates grace; and in fact, the different treatment of sacraments within Christianity is probably greater than the different treatment of sacraments between Christianity and New Age. This subject is discussed in greater detail in chapter 4.

AFTERLIFE Both religions believe in life after the death of the physical body; and although New Age has defined the afterlife more thoroughly than has Christianity, there can be no denial that a major foundation upon which each religion is built is the belief in an afterlife. This belief, incidentally, did not constitute a commonality which created the bridge between Judaism and

Christianity. This subject is discussed more thoroughly in Chapters 5-7.

THE PRESENCE OF GOD   Both religions believe in the presence of God, both in this life and in the afterlife. This is a major foundation for each religion, and tends to separate each from some of the older mystery religions in which ''mere mortals'' could never expect to be in the presence of God. This subject is presented in greater detail in Chapter 6.

MYSTERY RELIGIONS   Both religions started out as ''mystery religions'', so named because they represented secret cults into which individuals had to be initiated by passing certain secret and mysterious initiation tests or by participating in certain secret and mysterious initiation ceremonies. During various periods, the mystery religions have been successful because they have tended to offer the individual a way to feel a religious experience not provided by the official public religions. Christianity was considered to be a mystery religion prior to being personally accepted by the Roman Emperor Constantine in about 313 AD, and finally being declared the State Religion of the Roman Empire by Theodosius in 380 AD. Many consider New Age to be a mystery religion today. This subject is discussed in greater detail in essentially all of the subsequent chapters.

BELIEF IN THINGS UNSEEN   Both religions believe in the existence of things unseen. Christians are blessed if they believe without seeing [John 20:29] and some Christians believe in the existence of Angels. The New Agers believe in Angels, Archangels, and other beings or worlds whose multi-dimensional frequencies are beyond the sensory frequencies of human beings. This subject is discussed in greater detail in Chapters 5-7.

DIFFERENCES

TIME AND PHYSICAL FORM   Christians believe in a relatively short period of time during which man has been aware of God and that man's present physical form has been the main vehicle for soul incarnation; whereas New Agers believe that man has had a relationship with God, even on this physical plane or planet, for much longer than even scientists are willing to publicly admit, and that the soul has incarnated in physical forms unlike the present physical body even when on this physical planet. This subject is discussed in greater detail in several subsequent Chapters including 2, 5, and 6.

JESUS CHRIST   Christians believe that Jesus Christ is the only begotten Son of God and that God is approached only through him; whereas New Agers believe that although Jesus is divine and is one who has occupied the Office of the Christ, he has not been the only one. They thus believe that there are many avenues by which the Many Mansions of God may be approached without denying the divinity of Jesus, merely his exclusivity. This subject is discussed in greater detail in essentially all of the subsequent Chapters, particularly Chapter 7.

ORDINATION   The established Christian churches believe in clerical or priestly ordination only after formal education; whereas all New Agers, like some offspring Christian denominations, believe in priestly ordination based solely on committing their life to God and on their willingness to be tested. This subject is discussed further in Chapter 4.

DIMENSIONALITY   Most human beings believe in the three physical dimensions of length, height, and width and in the application of these three dimensions to the frequencies that we can see in the visible spectrum or hear in the audio frequency. They then apply this three-dimensional thought process to any religious sphere including Christianity. New Agers believe in multi-dimensional existences and apply this belief to physical objects, religious experiences and religious entities. And when New Agers refer to the fourth dimension, they do not necessarily mean Time as we understand it. Time is the commonly accepted fourth dimension in a three dimensional world. The subject of dimensionality is presented in greater detail in Chapter 5.

BODILY EXISTENCE Christians believe that they exist in the two bodies mentioned by Paul, the physical and the spiritual [1 Cor. 15:44], and that their existence on this physical plane occurs only once; whereas New Agers believe that they exist in physical, mental, emotional, and spiritual bodies and that they return to a variety of physical planes, including this planet, many times via reincarnation as directed by the Soul. These subjects are presented in all the subsequent Chapters.

ASCENSION Christians believe that Jesus ascended, and that all believers will bodily ascend after the Second Coming of the Christ; whereas New Agers believe that many Masters have ascended, that others are ascending all the time, that ascension is the natural result of the Soul's progress, that ascension will occur when the entity is ready, and that it is not vitally important whether or not the physical body presently being occupied is involved in the ascension process. This subject is discussed further in several of the subsequent chapters, with emphasis in Chapter 5.

ANGELS AND OTHER ENTITIES Although some Christians express a belief in Angels, and some Christian churches have designated certain entities as saintly beings through whom intercessory prayers may be made, the belief in such entities is merely a minor driving force within a major part of the Christian religion; whereas the existence of Archangels, Angels, Ascended Masters and other Extraterrestrials is one of the major driving forces within New Age. This subject is further addressed in all of the subsequent chapters.

REFERENCE WORKS Christians accept the Bible and ancillary works based on the Bible as their sole religious reference source; whereas New Agers accept other reference works in addition to the Bible. Among others, The Apocrypha, The Keys of Enoch, The Kabalah, the works on Edgar Cayce, or the works of Teilhard de Chardin and an increasing number of "channelers" would find favor among most followers of New Age. The succeeding chapters will use these and many other references as background material.

ORGANIZATION OF THE COSMOS Christians tend to believe in a Heaven and an Earth with very little else of any major religious importance in the universe; whereas New Agers believe in a heavily populated, well organized cosmos in which all activities have a religious purpose, even the regularity of planetary orbiting and interplanetary visitations. Additional detail on this subject will be found in Chapters 2, 5 and 6.

MISUNDERSTANDINGS

In addition to similarities and differences between Christianity and New Age Religion, there are misunderstandings between them. One major misunderstanding is related to religious dimensions in which the New Agers feel that Christianity is too narrow in its beliefs; whereas Christians feel that New Age is too shallow, fickle or inconsistent in theirs. An additional misunderstanding relates to the sincerity of each religion. Possibly one of the most articulate recent statements of this particular misunderstanding is presented in John Cornwell's book, The Hiding Places of God, published in October, 1991. In this book the author investigates thoroughly the mysticism associated with anything Roman Catholic, but speaks of New Age only in a chapter entitled "Satanism and the New Age". In this chapter the author strongly suggests that

New Age Religion invariably leads to Satanic cultism with its associated ceremonial acts of animal, child and sex abuse. There are ''saints and sinners'' in every religion; and there is no doubt that within the New Age movement, there are people who participate solely to satisfy their own Ego-related appetites, whether those appetites are related to sex, money or power. Such people also reside within the Christian church as evidenced by the recent activities of a Roman Catholic Archbishop in Atlanta and several former TV evangelists; or as evidenced by the historic activities of the Inquisition, several Popes, etc. These digressions do not negate the activities of the vast majority of Christians who are lead by the Spirit; and in a like manner, the digressions of some should not negate the activities of the many New Agers who are truly lead by the Spirit as they investigate their Way. Because New Age people investigate so many things, it may appear that some follow the Way of Darkness rather than Light; but that does not justify promoting the misunderstanding that all who follow New Age are worshippers of Satan whereas all who profess Christ are truly worshippers of God. Neither presumption is totally true. And neither presumption addresses the probability that in fact, a third group exists: the Satanists who are not a part of either, but who could be produced by either whenever the worship of Ego replaces the worship of God.

A final area of misunderstanding is that which often occurs as a natural part of human communication: *viz.* the mixing of emotional levels. Human communications reside on five emotional levels: Facts, Opinions, Attitudes, Values, and Beliefs. Trouble in communication will occur if the levels get mixed up. As an example, there can be no argument about Facts. Facts are Facts--period! They can be discussed, but they cannot be disputed or argued about. However, if one communicator states an Opinion as if it were a Fact, then the argument can really begin because a misunderstanding will have been created. A misunderstanding will always occur if the emotional levels get mixed up during commu-

29

nication. But these levels apply to more than just communication misunderstandings; they also relate to how Beliefs can become accepted by an individual. In any individual's life, out of many Facts, a few Opinions will be developed; out of many Opinions, some Attitudes will start to be seen; out of an Attitudinal base, some of life's Values will become established; out of which will come the ultimate in Faith--a few Beliefs. Thus, Facts can lead to Beliefs, but only through a long chain of intermediate development. Some misunderstandings are developing between Christians and New Agers because of Christianity's developed Beliefs vs. the emerging Beliefs of the New Age; and also because many Christians are evaluating statements from New Agers by asking for proof as if they were investigating Facts rather than hearing about Beliefs. As Christians and New Agers work together, it is hoped that these misunderstandings will become minimized or even disappear.

SUMMARY

There are many similarities, differences and misunderstandings which exist between Christianity as it is being practiced by its adherents today, and New Age as it is being practiced by its adherents today. Within the New Age movement, all degrees of emphasizing the similarities, differences or misunderstandings can be found. Some New Age adherents have taken the extreme route of completely turning their back on the established church and its religious practices. In this degree of emphasis they are acting like the Essenes of some two thousand years ago. Other New Age adherents have taken the other extreme of following the practice of the Christian church while giving only lip service to New Age beliefs. This is somewhat like being one of the Christian Jews for whom Hebrews was written--they want the new religion while holding on to all the laws, traditions, and teachings of their parent religion. Between those extremes are people who accept the good of Christianity while sincerely believing that man's influence has made this once-sacred religion too limiting. They may be found in the established church, teaching the reality of Christianity including the divinity of Jesus the Christ. In addition, they may be found within the New Age group meetings, learning of the reality of religious experiences which expand beyond those mentioned in the established churches.

The subsequent Chapters go into greater detail about the similarities, differences and misunderstandings between Christianity and New Age. As the New Age practitioner expands his understanding of Christianity and the Christian practitioner expands his understanding of New Age, it is hoped that a merger will occur which presents a continuance even more successful than that represented by the Judeo-Christian heritage.

''Know what it is to be a child? It is to be something very different from the man of today. It is to have a spirit yet streaming from the waters of baptism; it is to **believe** in love, to **believe** in loveliness, to **believe in belief**; it is to be so little that the elves can reach to whisper in your ear; it is to turn pumpkins into coaches; and mice into horses, lowness into loftiness, and nothing into everything, for each child has its fairy godmother in its soul.''

Francis Thompson *Shelley. In The Dublin Review*
[July, 1908]

''Be not afraid of life. **Believe** that life is worth living, and your **belief** will help create the fact.''

William James *The Will to Believe* [1897]. *Is Life Worth Living?*

CHAPTER 2   BELIEF IN GOD

All religions have a belief in "something". Quite often, that "something" is recognized as the creator and governor of the universe. In fact, that belief is a major part of the accepted definition of the word "religion". Generally, the "something" which is believed in is called "God", again because of the accepted definition of that particular word. As an act of belief, all religions will have some sort of a defined relationship between themselves and their God. The study of this defined relationship is called "theology", a study about the nature of God and religious truth, including the relationship between mankind and God. Finally, it is an historical fact that when a number of like-thinking people study their brand of theology in order to understand the nature of the God which created them, they band together. This is a very natural human reaction. This banding together creates a religious sect which in turn establishes a religion. If these like-thinking people who have banded together have a different view of the nature of God than had previously been proposed by others, then the religion which they establish would be thought of as a new religion.

But through all of this, there are three characteristics about

33

the people who become a part of their religion: [1] they believe in a creator whom they try to designate by name; [2] they worship that creator with adoration, testimony and submission; and [3] they study and work in order to understand their relationship with that creator. These characteristics persist whether the religion is old or new.

The purpose of this chapter is to compare Christianity and New Age by looking at several aspects of the belief each has in its creator. These aspects include names, definitions, functions, relationships, plans and the like.

THE NAMES OF GOD

The Revised Standard Version [RSV] of the Bible is the version used by many Christians. Although there are many other versions of the Bible, today the RSV is generally accepted as the authorized Bible in the English language. In this Bible, the fourth word is "God", as "In the beginning God created the heavens and the earth [Gen. 1:1]". Thus, very early it is established for most Christians that in the English language, their creator is to be called "God". In the RSV, the name of the creator is invariably God, or Lord, or sometimes Lord God.

The RSV was undertaken in 1870 by authority of the Church of England. This version and the corresponding American Standard Version have been continually upgraded in order to have the meanings of the words used in the RSV correspond as closely as possible with current, accepted word usage. The RSV was required because by the mid-nineteenth century, advances in biblical study and newly found ancient manuscripts had shown that the previous widely used version of the Bible, the King James Version [KJV] had serious defects. The KJV had been in use as the generally accepted Bible since its publication in 1611. It had been based on some seven previous versions published between about

1530 and 1582. These versions had varied so greatly in their content that a royal commission was created to sort out the mess. After some spirited competition with the Geneva Bible of 1560, the KJV became accepted for over 250 years as the authorized Bible in the English language. Much of the KJV, particularly the New Testament, owes its origin to the Tyndale Bible published in about 1530. The Tyndale Bible was the first English-language Bible translated directly from the original Hebrew and Greek rather than from Latin as was the Church-dictated requirement at that time. Because it had not been translated from Latin, the established church authorities ordered the Tyndale Bible to be designated as an ''untrue translation'' and to be burned. In 1536, the author, William Tyndale, also was burned--at the stake. So much for Christian charity.

This history needs to be understood because, in addition to correcting the defects in the KJV, the RSV simplified the words of the Bible. As one example of simplification, instead of using a variety of names for God, the RSV uses only ''God'' or ''Lord'' or [rarely] ''Lord God'' as titles, and sometimes ''deity'' as a reference. In contrast, the KJV used a variety of names for God, such as: God, Godhead, God-who-forgives, God-who-sees, God-most-high, YAH, Yahweh, Jehovah, and the like. In this manner, the KJV follows closely the Hebrew texts which also use a variety of names for God, such as: Elohim, ha-Elohim, Jehovah [or Yahweh], Jehovah-Elohim, El Shaddai, and the like.

As another example of simplification, it might be useful to compare the poetic KJV and the more easily understood RSV by examining a single verse such as Romans 1:20. The KJV says: ''For the invisible things of him from the creation of the world are clearly seen, being understood by the things that are made, even his eternal power and Godhead''; whereas the RSV says: ''Ever since the creation of the world, his invisible nature, namely his eternal power and deity, has been clearly perceived in the things that have been made''. The RSV has obviously been simplified and thus is easier to understand.

As a final example, it might be useful to examine how the variety of Hebrew-source names has been simplified by the RSV. The RSV version of Exodus 6:2-3 reads, ''.... And God said to Moses, 'I am the Lord. I appeared to Abraham, to Isaac, and to Jacob, as God Almighty, but by my name the Lord I did not make myself known to them.' ''; whereas the use of Hebrew names would read, ''....And Elohim spake unto Moses and said unto him, ' I am Jehovah; and I appeared unto Abraham, unto Isaac, and unto Jacob as El Shaddai; but by my name Jehovah, I was not known to them.' '' Again, the RSV has simplified the text by making it more readable and easily understood.

And so, the RSV has simplified and clarified the words of the KJV, even to the point of omitting the various names for God which might have different shades of interpretation or meaning. The various names of God may have been more nearly correct at the time of the original writing, and may even be more nearly correct today. However, the Bible is a book, and all books are written by man with one major purpose in mind-- that of communication. And although inspired by God, the books of the Bible have been chosen by, assembled by, written by, and translated and retranslated by man in an attempt to communicate. The use of the accepted words ''God'' or ''Lord'' does not seem to be too high a price to pay for enhanced communication and reduced confusion even if shades of meaning might have been lost in the process. The goals of enhanced communication and reduced confusion have been effectively accomplished by the Revised Standard Version of the Bible.

In summary, the tendency in Christianity today is to use the words ''God'' or ''Lord'' when referring to the deity whom they worship and adore. In addition, Christians tend to follow the first commandment of their Judeo-Christian heritage by having no other deity before Him. The name of their creator is God or Lord. And that is the end of that!

New Agers use a number of names for their deity. The deepest thinkers tend to use the Tetragrammaton. The Tetragrammaton is four Hebrew letters, usually transliterated as YHWH or JHWH and used as a symbol for the ineffable name of God. These four consonants could, of course, not be pronounced as a word without adding some vowels such as in Yahweh or Jehovah. Pronounced as four consonants, they would be Yod Hey Vod Hey; but in reality, this is merely the pronunciation of four letters, not the making of a word or name. By the use of the Tetragrammaton, the name of the creator remains ineffable, which means that it is beyond expression or unspeakable. It symbolizes the one who cannot be named. To go farther, New Agers consider their YHWH to be the YodHeyVodHey of the Living Everlasting Light, the Living God behind all the Creator Gods. Finally, ''YHWH'' is one of the seventy-two sacred names of the Infinite Mind, each having its own Father universe and celestial Hierarchy [see Chapters 2 and 6]. The basis for this deep thinking is presented in The Keys of Enoch and in other such literature.

In addition, New Agers might use the word God when referring to their creator, but rarely without letting all know that this God is not solely the masculine or neuter God which seems to constitute most of the Judeo-Christian heritage. Instead, the New Ager will refer to Mother-Father God, one in which all duality has become one; one in which the below of the Mother Earth has merged on an equal basis with the above of the Father Heaven in a way that fulfills the promise of ''as above, so below''; one that brings into oneness the duality of all created beings; one which uses the oneness to be in the presence of the oneness of God. The New Age religion tends to emphasize the dual nature within the oneness of God, including the equality of the female part of that dual nature of oneness, to an extent not practiced since some of the ancient Mystery Religions, and way beyond any feminine participation in the masculine or neuter nature of God as expressed by Judaism, Christianity, Islam, or the other more "modern" religions.

Furthermore, New Agers will call on the names of creator gods who function under the will of the Living God. Some of these are the Elihom who are identified as the Creator God in the original Hebrew texts and who are also identified by the New Ager as the Creator Divinities under YHWH. They control the calibrations of Light necessary to create. Thus, these creator gods created this world and continue to create other worlds by the will of YHWH. The word Elihom appears over 2,500 times in the Hebrew writings of the Old Testament. Prior to Enoch's appearance in the Bible, the word was always "Elihom" because the only god identified was the creator god who remained hidden after man was driven out of the Garden of Eden. However, the first time that God walked with man as He did with Enoch [Gen. 5:22], He was "ha-Elihom" meaning "revealed Creator". Later, when He appeared to Abraham [Gen. 17:2], He was "El Shaddai" meaning God Almighty as He had been when He was represented by Melchizedek [Gen 14:18]. By the time of His appearance on Mt. Sinai [Ex. 19:17] where He presented the Ten Commandments [Ex. 20:1], He had become "Yahweh" [or Jehovah], the spoken version of YHWH. Because of this sequence, the New Ager believes that the Elohim, who are the Creator Divinities, become identified with YHWH, the Living God by whose will and under whose direction and in whose name the Creator Divinities made all that is. There are names for these Creator Divinities, just as there are names for others who help YHWH. Some New Agers tend to give adoration to or to seek help from some of the members at the hierarchical level represented by these Creator Divinities or their helpers; while others find their comfort solely at the foot of the Living God behind the Creator Divinities-- the Living Everlasting Light represented by the name that cannot be said, the Tetragrammatron transliterated to YHWH.

The Revised Standard Version of the Bible makes no distinction between the God of Genesis 1:1 who created the heaven and the earth, the God of Genesis 5:22 who revealed Himself by walking with Enoch, or the "Top God" of Exodus 20:1 who gave His people the Ten Commandments. This may represent the desire to communicate more readily just as modern authors have been taught to simplify their presentations in order to communicate their ideas more readily. But it does seem as if a fuller understanding has been sacrificed on the altar of efficient communications if both the God who first gave the commandment that "You shall have no other Gods before me" and the Creator Divinities who followed His will to create heaven and earth are designated by the same name. The RSV makes no distinction between these two; whereas the original Hebrew texts certainly seem to, and so does the New Ager.

But the major point to be communicated during this discussion is that whether it is the Christian who uses the same word, God, in referring to the Creator who made all things and also to the Giver of the Ten Commandments before whom there is no other God; or whether it is the New Ager who involves an organization of hierarchical beings who perform functions under the will of the Living God before whom there is no other although under whom there may be many, the intent is the same. That intent is in the belief that there is one Being who rules heaven and earth and all else, and that Being, whether called God, I AM, YHWH, or something else which cannot be pronounced is the One to whom Adoration, Honor, Commitment, Love, Testimony, and Submission is due.

In <u>Romeo and Juliet</u> Act I, Scene II, Shakespeare writes, " What's in a name? That which we call a rose by any other name would smell as sweet." And so it is with the argument which goes on and on about what is the name of God. As long as we humans pay homage to the One who has created us and thus has a claim upon us, then we are as loved as the child who pays homage to its parents, whether by calling them mother, father, mom, pop, ma, dad, ma'am, sir, or friend. And although some New Agers believe in Mantras, or in the vibrational energies which come from repeating certain names or sounds, that is merely an aid, not the principle method for making contact with the One. That principle method is through prayer and meditation, both in Christianity and in New Age.

Like other religious beings, Christians and New Agers have tried to find a name for their Creator. Although the names chosen may be different, any real difference between the Christians and the New Agers on this issue is, at worst, so minor as to be ignored by anyone who has an open heart and mind.

THE DEFINITIONS OF GOD

In 1927, Werner Heisenberg, a German physicist and philosopher articulated a principle of sub-atomic physics which stated that the velocity and the position of a particle could not be precisely measured at the same time; and that the more closely one tries to determine either the velocity or the position of a particular particle, the more uncertain the determination of the other parameter will become. This phenomenon has absolutely nothing to do with any inadequacy in the instruments, the techniques or the talents applied to the measurement; instead it has to do with the intimate relationship between particles and waves on the sub-atomic level. But the meaning to physics was even more profound than its founding example, for it revealed that no matter how hard we might try, there will be things which will remain uncertain.

The Uncertainty Principle was developed for use in the physical field of atomic physics in which it has continued to prove to be extremely useful. However, that particular usefulness is not the point of this discussion. Instead, the point to be made is that the Uncertainty Principle has also proved to be extremely useful when applied to the non-physical field of metaphysics. One particular example of this application would be the probability that the more precisely one would try to define God, the more uncertain one would be that the definition would have any usefulness whatsoever.

Nevertheless, since the beginning of the human experience, people have tried to define God. Questions have been asked such as "What is God?" or "Who is God?". Philosophers, theologians, and even common folk have tried to answer these questions. But to do so can be somewhat like trying to understand what electricity is. There is an old story about the time that Einstein was taking a walk on the campus of Princeton University and met a young, freshman electrical engineer. During the ensuing conversation, the world-famous scientist asked the nervous freshman what electricity was, and received the stuttering reply of, "Gosh, Professor, I knew what is was last night, but I seem to have forgotten." Einstein immediately slapped the palm of his hand against his forehead and replied, "Oh mein Gott, imagine that. The only person in the world who has ever known what electricity is has forgotten it!". For you see, we cannot truly define electricity. We have no real knowledge about what electricity is, only what it does! And although in all practical terms this statement could also be used to describe our knowledge about God, we would not be inquisitive humans if we did not continue to try to define Him.

Christians, of course, will look to the Bible for their definition, but they will be disappointed, for far from defining or even proving God's existence, the Bible simply takes the existence of God for granted, and gives rather skimpy definitions of who or what He is. The early part of the Bible, in which the word "God" is used the most often, primarily describes what He did. As a few examples, in the first 1.3% of the Old Testament, He made heaven, earth, light, firmament, water, dry land, plants, all living creatures, and mankind in His image; then He further established rules for mankind's obedience, destroyed the earth by flood, made promises to Abraham and to Jacob, destroyed Sodom and Gomorrah, etc. etc. etc. But it is not until reaching the Song of Moses in the 15th Chapter of Exodus, some 6% of the Old Testament later, that the first rather inadequate descriptions of God appear. This happens when this ancient poem says, ''Lord, who among the gods is like you? Who is like you, wonderful in holiness? Who can work miracles and mighty acts like yours?...You, Lord, will be king forever and ever.'' And so we have the first definitions of God in the hints that He is unique, powerful and eternal. Prior to that He had been an undefined <u>doer</u>!

Later, the Old Testament implies that God is invisible, is not a natural force, is not an abstraction, is active in showing His love, power, and justice, and is a personal God. But other than these attributes, God is never really described or defined. This should not be too surprising, for if God is greater than the sum total of all human intelligence and experiences, He should be indescribable and indefinable. We should not be able to define Him because He should be beyond all our experiences. He should be ineffable.

But the limited definitions of God in the Bible have not kept mankind from trying to develop more complete or at least more understandable definitions. As a result, along with other things, modern Christian theology has defined God in three ways: by the ''alls'', the ''persons'', and the ''oneness''.

The ''alls'' refer to the definition of God which says that He is omnipotent [having <u>all</u> power], omniscient [having <u>all</u> knowledge], and omnipresent [being in <u>all</u> places]. Prior to Judaism, many religions had felt that their gods had great levels of knowledge and power; and some religions had even proposed that there was only one god. But the YHWH of the Old Testament was unique in that He, and only He of all the gods proposed up until that time, was in all places. Many prior religions had their god residing in a statue, or in a living animal, or at some specific spot someplace up in the mountains, or at least at some physical place to which an individual might [or might not] go; but no one had proposed a god who was everywhere, a god who was in all places. And so, the God of Christianity is the One who has all of the "alls".

The term "persons" refers to "God in three persons, Blessed Trinity". Although the final definition of the Trinity was not accepted by the Church for several hundred years, the possibility of its existence in some form has been a part of Christianity since the introduction of the Holy Spirit on the Day of Pentecost [Acts 2:1-4], a day which is generally considered to be the real founding of the Christian Church. The Trinity is composed of God the Father, God the Son, and God the Holy Spirit. It is a concept which has confused many people; but according to Christians, it should not. It is merely that within the nature of the one eternal God, there are three distinct Persons: the Father, the son and the Holy Spirit. These three Persons are the one God.[3] In John Cornwell's non-fiction book The Hiding Places of God, another interpretation is expressed when Sister Briege McKenna, a Catholic nun who is a real person states, "If you believe, as I do, that our bodies, our minds, our souls are one entity, it stands to reason that the healing of the body might follow from a spiritual healing."[4] The pertinent part of this quotation is not related to healing, but instead to the fact that a trained Catholic nun believes that we as individuals have three "bodies", a physical body, a mental body, and a spiritual body all within this one entity which we call a human. And so, the concept of there being three "persons" within one entity known as God is not too difficult. It merely suggests that like us, God exists in three bodies: the mental [God the Father who is the Infinite Mind]; the spiritual [God the Holy Spirit who was given to His earthly followers on the Day of Pentecost]; and the physical [God, the Son who was incarnated as Jesus, the Christ]. And so the God of Christianity is the One who exists in three ''persons'' or ''bodies'' within One.

The ''oneness'' is a concept which is accepted by many, but not necessarily all Christians. It is a concept which is found in a number of Biblical references. From the Old Testament, a prime reference on oneness might be Genesis 1:27 which says ''So God created man in his own image, in the image of God he created him; male and female he created them''. Thus we have the oneness of God being expressed as an ''image'' containing the duality of male and female within the One. From the New Testament, three references on oneness might be: [1] John 10:30 in which Jesus says ''I and the Father are one''; [2] John 4:24 in which Jesus says ''God is a spirit and those who worship him must worship in spirit and truth''; and [3] Luke 17:21 in which Jesus says '' ...for behold, the kingdom of God is within you''. These, and other New Testament teachings such as the Parable of the Prodigal Son [Luke 15:11-32], propose that when an entity such as one of us can find his way back to God, the God which we meet will be one with whom we will find as much ''oneness'' as any returning son can find with his father. It is the oneness of identity, of companionship and of purpose. Although this is not much of a definition, it does imply that we and God are only an acceptance apart from oneness with each other-- only an acceptance apart from being like each other in many ways. And so, the Christian God is the One who can make us like Him if we will only accept Him.

In conclusion, despite all of these efforts a Christian does not have much of a definition of his God. But then, how do you define the indefinable or effable the ineffable? The answer is that you don't; but we will probably keep on trying!

The New Ager is in exactly the same boat as his Christian brother, for the New Ager has no definition of the Infinite Mind either. However, the New Ager does have a belief in the many functions performed by the One, and these functions do start to present a functional definition of the Infinite Mind. Functional definitions are not all that bad. For example, if one were to be asked, "Who are you?" and were to answer by saying, "I am an Electrical Engineer", he would have helped to define something functional about himself. And although the asker would not have received a real definition, he at least would know more than he had known before. He might not know who the person is, but he might know a little about what the person does. In this way, functional definitions can be useful. But before such functional definitions can be developed, the functions have to be understood; for there is absolutely no purpose in knowing that someone is an Electrical Engineer if you haven't the foggiest idea what an electrical engineer is or does. And so the New Ager will need to present some functional understanding before his God will start to be described by some functional definitions.

THE FUNCTIONS OF GOD

From the beginning, people have pondered the mystery of creation. They ask, "Where did I come from?", or "Why am I here", or "Who created God?". They become amazed and enchanted at the physical arrangement of a giraffe or an elephant; they become awed by the grandeur of the Rocky Mountains or the Grand Canyon; they become entranced by technology. In all of this, they wonder if they are alone in the Universe. They search for answers in their Bible or in other religious works. In Genesis, they read of the Creation and thrill at the wonder of it all. In Job, they find that Job is in awe at the power of God and they also become awed at the power of one who could be responsible for all that exists. But then a major truth descends upon them. They realize that with the possible exception of the Creation, the Bible does not attempt to prove the existence of God by stating what He does, but instead merely presents the joy of those who live in the presence of Him as contrasted to the despair of those who do not. Other than His love and a few other less meaningful attributes, the Bible leaves in abeyance the question of whether or not there is a God and what He does with His time. And so, in the absence of a Biblical presentation of the functions of God, the Christian is left with trying to understand a God whose functions could range all the way from those functions presented by Deism on one extreme to those presented by Determinism on the other.

Deism was the religious attitude expressed by many of the Western world's intellectual leaders from the latter part of the 17th century into the early part of the 19th century. Its five principles were considered to be God-given and innate in the mind of man from the beginning of time. They were possessed by the first man and thus owed nothing to the priests or clerics of the established churches. These principles were articulated by Edward Herbert [later 1st Baron Herbert of Cherbury] as the following:

1. A belief in a supreme being;
2. A need to worship that being;
3. A pursuit of a pious and virtuous life as the most desired way to worship that being;
4. A need to repent sins; and
5. A belief in an afterlife at which reward or punishment would be administered.

Many of the Founding Fathers of the American Republic were Deists. Among others, Benjamin Franklin, George Washington, John Adams, and Thomas Jefferson were acknowledged Deists, based primarily on their correspondence rather than on their declarations, for Deism was more a state of mind and belief than a professed identification. Many influential and intellectual English, French and Germans also were Deists. Some of the more notable were the Earl of Shaftesbury, Voltaire, Gottfried Wilhelm Leibniz, etc. Deism was an important contributor to the religious principles of what Will Durant has described as "The Age of Reason" during which man was first led to think things out for himself rather than blindly following the dictates of those who led the established churches. Deism implied that man could reason out things for himself instead of receiving knowledge through revelation or through the teachings of any church. Deists did believe in Christ, but felt that His teachings were not novel. Instead, they were as old as creation, a republication of primitive monotheism in which Christ would have had to be a part. They thus affirmed Christ's presence since the creation. By this affirmation, the Deists could be considered to be Christian.

As Deism developed, one important tenet was that God was not involved in the world in any significant way other than to create it and set the laws of it. He then would leave it alone to continue in its own way. Thus, anything that happened in the world was man's doing and his doing alone. He would be rewarded or punished in the next world based on what he did in this world; but to expect God to intervene in the affairs of man would have been completely foreign to the beliefs of the Deists. They saw the function of God as the creator and as nothing else. Deists were the epitome of free-will thinking, *i.e.* that man had not only the right, but the obligation to decide things entirely by himself and for himself by using solely his own free will. The Deist would never say, "Thy will be done" because God does not have a will in this world. He merely created the world, and then left its running to us.

The exact opposite of Deism is Determinism. The Determinists believe that all events, including moral choices, are determined by previously existing causes. Therefore, there is no free will and the future of everything has already been determined. And although Determinism is a philosophical rather than a religious concept, it has had a tremendous influence on many religious practices. As examples, Determinism was very important to pre-reformed Islam, to medieval Judaism, and to the Christian doctrine of ''double predestination'' which was presented by the Synod of Dort [Reformed church movement] and which was further mentioned in the writings of St. Augustine and Martin Luther and in the thinking of the Jansenists. This particular doctrine states that God has determined from eternity whom He will save and whom He will damn, regardless of their abiding faith, love or merit, or regardless of their lack of any of these desirable qualities. That is Determinism in spades! As a religious person, a Determinist would never say, ''Thy will be done'', because he would believe that it would be done in our lives whether we give God that invitation by submitting ourselves to Him or not.

The Deists and the Determinists represent the two extremes of Christian thought in relation to God's functions. In the first case, God has no function other than to create, leave things alone, and evaluate what has happened. God has no will in what is done in our lives; instead it is entirely our own free will to do as we choose. In the second case, God has all the functions and has chosen to use them throughout eternity. Man has no free will; it is only God's will. Because of this, all has already been decided for man and he can change nothing, no matter how hard he would try.

The major portion of Christian theology in relation to the functions of God resides between these two extremes. In general, most of this theology tends to follow the guidelines expressed in Romans 8:28, ''We know that in everything, God works for good with those who love Him, who are called according to his purpose''. In this philosophy, both free will and God's will have a place. It is man's free will to decide whether or not to love God, and then to commit himself to being called to do God's purpose. If he does, then it is God's will to work for good both to and through the one who used his free will to choose God's way. If, on the other hand, it is man's free will to decide to avoid God's love and will, then God will do nothing other then to wait patiently for His child to decide to return to Him and His will. This is the prime message contained in the Eden story [Genesis Chapter 3] and in the parable of the Prodigal Son as contrasted to the parables of the Lost Sheep and the Lost Coin [Luke Chapter 15].

And so to the Christian, God's functions are: to create heaven and earth and all therein including mankind in His own image; to wait patiently until each of His children returns to Him of his own free will; to work for good with and through His children who have returned; and through Christ, to bring His children unto Himself so that where He is, they may be also [John 14:3]. To help describe the One who would perform these functions, the Christian would say that He is omniscient, omnipotent, omnipresent, loving, caring, kind and patient. He is the Father.

To the New Ager, the functions of God are more like that of a benevolent CEO in that He manages things in a very kind manner and through a hierarchy of beings who help Him. The New Ager believes that the Infinite Mind oversees a number of Universes. Some New Agers propose that there are some seventy two Universes, each under the direction of an entity who was created in the image of God long before homo sapiens walked on the face of the Earth. These ancient beings oversee several Sectors within their Universe. Each Sector is governed by another entity who, with the help of many Ascended Masters and angels, directs the overall activities of his Sector. These activities include a plan for the progress of each entity who resides in the Sector. As a part of that plan, the Akashic Records are reviewed, Karma is placed or erased, and the next incarnation, either progressive or regressive is defined and placed into motion. After that incarnation is in motion, the free will of the incarnated entity becomes involved in that it may decide to follow the Way, or it may decide not to, at which time the plan is put into abeyance until returned to by the free will choice of the entity. For those who follow the Way, the phrase, ''Thy will be done'' becomes a vital admission of God's presence in their life, as well as their free will acceptance of His Way. And "followers of the Way" becomes another tie-in between Christians and New Agers in that in the early days, Christians were known as "belonging to the Way" before they were known as Christians [Acts 9:2].

And so, the New Ager believes that God's functions are many, in that the Infinite Mind is behind all of the strategy and tactics for the progression of every Soul on every Celestial Body in every Sector in every Universe. To help describe the One who would perform these functions, the New Ager would say that He is very very Big, very very Wise, very very Kind, very very Understanding, and very very Very! He is the All.

THE RELATIONSHIPS WITH GOD

If there is any merit in naming, defining or understanding the functions of God, that merit pales into insignificance in comparison with understanding the relationship between God and mankind which, after all, is the prime purpose for establishing any religion.

The relationship of a Christian with his God is probably best defined by the 14th Chapter of John, starting with verse 6 and selectively continuing thereafter as follows:

Jesus said to him, "I am the way, and the truth, and the life; no one comes to the Father, but by me. If you had known me, you would have known my Father also; henceforth you will know him and have seen him." Philip said to him, "Lord, show us the Father, and we will be satisfied." Jesus said to him, "Have I been with you so long and yet you do not know me, Philip? He who has seen me has seen the Father: how can you say, 'Show us the Father?' Do you not believe that I am in the Father and the Father in me?"..."Truly, truly, I say to you, he who believes in me will also do the works that I do; and greater works than these will he do because I go to the Father''....Jesus answered him, '' If a man loves me, he will keep my word, and my Father will love him, and we will come to him and make our home with him. He who does not love me does not keep my words; and the word which you hear is not mine, but the Father's who sent me.''...''Peace I leave with you; my peace I give to you; not as the world gives do I give you. Let not your hearts be troubled, neither let them be afraid''...''I will no longer talk much with you, for the ruler of this world is coming. He has no power over me, but I do as the Father has commanded me, so that the world may know that I love the Father.''

Another clue about a Christian's relationship with his God is found in Luke 17:20-21 which says: Being asked by the Pharisees when the kingdom of God was coming, he [Jesus] answered them, ''The kingdom of God is not coming with signs to be observed; nor will they say, 'Lo, here it is!' or 'There!' for behold, the kingdom of God is within you.'' Most Biblical scholars believe that the word used by Jesus in this statement is the Aramaic word ''malkutha'' which is more correctly translated ''kingship'' rather than ''kingdom''.[5] Thus, Jesus was saying that the kingship of God is within you. He was not referring to territorial space.

And so the relationship that a Christian has with his God is one which comes through Christ who is one with the Father. It is a relationship of love and of peace. It is a relationship not of this world, but of a home which God makes by installing the Godly kingship or power within the one who loves Him. It is a relationship worthy of being developed.

The New Ager has a relationship with his God which is somewhat similar to that experienced by the Christian, but one in which certain relationship arrangements are different and one in which other parts of the relationship are emphasized to a much greater degree. As one example of a different relationship arrange-

51

ment, in the "kingship within", the spiritual New Age entity feels that not only does he honor God by addressing prayers to Him, God also honors the entity by visiting with him and residing within him. Thus, the relationship becomes more nearly a two-way street than that which is presented by Christianity. As another example, the New Ager feels that his God needs his help in order to accomplish certain things in either the physical or etheric realms of this planet. He contributes this help by meditation, or by setting up specific vibrational frequencies, or by experiencing growth along the Way. By growing and making progress along the Way, New Agers feel that they are pulling every other entity in the universe along with them. Consequently, all move closer to God by growth. And by this growth, God also grows and expands. Thus, both have been helped by the progress of those on the Way. Again, this two-way street of helping each other is not emphasized in Christianity.

As one example of a major difference in relationships, whereas the Christian feels that his relationship with God can happen only through Jesus the Christ, the New Ager feels that Jesus was only one of the many who have been anointed to fill the "Office of the Christ", and that this Office has been in existence since the beginning of time as has the Christ. Consequently, in the reference in which Jesus says, "No one comes to the Father but by me" [John 14:6], the New Ager believes that the reference is to the Office of the Christ of which Jesus was a recent occupant and not necessarily to Jesus the person. The New Ager believes that all must come through the portal of the Office of the Christ in order to reach the Father and arrive at "the many rooms of God" [John 14:2]. In this way, the New Ager believes in the divinity and eternality of the Christ, but not in the exclusivity of Jesus.[6] As another example of a major difference, the New Ager feels that he has had a relationship with his God which has covered an extremely long period of time and which has encompassed many incarnations in many different physical forms and that the reference which states that "And just as it is appointed for men to die once, and after that comes judgment'' [Hebrews 9:27], refers to the soul or spiritual body and not to the physical body. Reincarnation involves the use of many physical bodies for the incarnation of the soul in order to enable the soul to have a multitude of experiences. It is one of the major tenets of the New Age and is addressed further in Chapters 5-7. For the past 1450 years, the concept of reincarnation has been ignored by the established Christian church despite Biblical references which suggest this concept, and early Christian writings which state the reality of the concept. These latter writings are Apocrypha, and were not accepted by those who believed they followed God's guidance by establishing church doctrine and ecclesiastical law.

And so, the New Ager sees his relationship with God as being somewhat similar to that experienced by the Christian. However, the New Ager feels that his relationship is much nearer to a two-way street, that it is available through many channels only a recent one of which is represented by Jesus the Christ, and that it has been going on for a much longer time than the Christian would ever care to admit. Again, these subjects are addressed further in Chapters 5-7.

THE PLANS OF GOD

From the time that man first started to worship God, he has asked, ''What does God have in store for me?'' Later, when families were established, he asked, '' What does God have in store for me and mine?'' Then when tribes and later nations came into existence, man asked, '' What does God have in store for us?'' And it is highly likely that when man finds that he is not alone in this universe, he will ask, ''What does God plan to do about all this?'' For one of the prime hopes in establishing a relationship with God is the desire to become timeless like God and thus to be able to know what is going to happen in the future.

What are God's plans? That is the question for all time; that is the search which is a part of all religions; that is the hope for all mankind, for most people do hope that God has a plan. That hope is a belief which keeps man going. And most also believe that if man just knew how, he could find out what that plan was. Man must believe this, else why would there be so much interest in the reading of tea leaves, chicken entrails, and star or planet interactions? Man must want this, else why would there be so much interest in the prophecies of Nostradamus, of Cagliostro, of The National Enquirer, of the Bible? Man must know that he shouldn't have this, else why would he want it so badly?

The Christian will look for his insight into the future by examining the major prophesies contained in the Bible, and there are many major prophesies presented in the Bible. A recent book presents an index containing almost 1600 scriptural references to 37 major prophesies These prophesies cover The Prophetic Chart of Human Destiny and range from the first prophecy of Sin and Death to the final prophecy of the New Heaven and the New Earth. But many of these prophecies cover events which have already happened or which are a part of a Christian's religious heritage. Not all of them apply to what God's plan for His people might be now! If you were to ask a studious Christian what he believes to be God's plan for His people today, he would most probably reply, "The Second Coming of Christ and the consequent Millennial Kingdom" or maybe just "The Coming of the Kingdom", for to a Christian, this describes his belief of God's present plan to a greater extent than any other possible answer. And, of course, there is a great deal of reference to this plan in the Bible.

The precise phrase "the second coming of Christ" is never mentioned as such in the Bible. Instead, there are references to the purpose of Christ's first coming and to the promise that He will appear again. As an example, Hebrews 9:28 says, "so Christ, having been offered once to bear the sins of many, will appear a second time, not to deal with sin but to save those who are eagerly waiting for him.'' Since those who wait for the Lord are waiting for the establishment of His Kingdom, then the two comings of Christ are well defined: the first to take away sin and the second to have all become subjective to the Christ as King of Kings and Lord of Lords in His Kingdom. This is the major message about the comings of Christ as presented in both the Old and the New Testaments. To the Christian, therefore, God's plan is the Coming of the Kingdom which is heralded by the appearance of Jesus the Christ.

The word ''millennium'' originally meant 1,000 years. Thus, to the Christian the ''Millennial Kingdom'' has always literally meant the kingdom over which Christ would rule for 1,000 years. But because the Millennial Kingdom was looked forward to with such great desire, the word millennium has developed a new definition: that which means a hoped-for period of joy, serenity, prosperity and justice. This definition has no reference to any specific amount of time and therefore can have absolutely no relationship to the origin of the word ''millennium'' which comes from Latin and simply means ''thousand'' [mille] ''year'' [annus as related to biennium for ''two years'']. This new definition is therefore the direct result of the understanding of God's plan as visualized by the Christian.

According to the Revelation to John [the Apocalypse], the Millennial Kingdom will be established by the destruction of the armies gathered against God in the Holy Land, by the capture of the Beast and the False Prophet, by the binding of Satan, and by the resurrection of the martyred dead of the Tribulation so that they can reign with Christ. According to Isaiah, in the Millennial Kingdom, God's chosen people of Israel will be exalted above all others; and although the Gentiles will have a major place, they will be second to Israel in their spiritual blessing. However, according to Isaiah this will not be too bad because the spiritual life of the Kingdom will be like none before it, since all who inhabit the Kingdom will be without sin from the first day and therefore their spiritual study will be much more productive. Isaiah also says that there will be no weapons of war, and therefore all taxes can be used to bring about justice and equality of abundance for all. Ezekiel and Jeremiah also predict abundance, and Ezekiel and Zachariah predict a vast change in the topography of Palestine with a large river flowing south from an elevated Jerusalem. During the thousand years of the Kingdom [literal interpretation], the human history of the present Earth will end, and the glory of the Kingdom will be eclipsed by the New Heaven, the New Earth, and the New Jerusalem. But this will happen only after one final conflict between God and Satan who by this time has become unbound but who is finally to be put out of commission.

The specific signs or events which indicate that the Kingdom is at hand are carefully recorded in the Bible; however they are so subject to interpretation that the End has been predicted often over the past two thousand years. In particular, the 2nd, the 7th, the 11th, the 14th and the early part of the 20th centuries were all singled out at the time as possessing all the signs of the impending Armageddon [i.e. the final battle between the forces of good and evil], including an identified Beast, a known False Prophet and the like. So powerful have been these predictions that an entire segment of theology named "eschatology" has been established to handle them. The word "eschatology" comes from several Greek words which mean "ideas about the end", and many churches or religions are very eschatological in their beliefs. In Jesus' time, the Essenes and even Jesus himself were strong in their belief that the end was at hand, meaning that the Millennium was coming soon!

And so, the Christian believes that God's plan involves the establishment of a perfect Kingdom, initiated by the physical appearance of Christ and terminated by the humans of the Earth leaving it to become a part of the New Jerusalem which will exist in eternity. But although many have tried, none can state exactly when this will occur. And although many may have tried to improve mankind in the hope that God's plan might become better or come sooner, most Christians believe in a set plan in which they, but not necessarily any other part of mankind, will participate.

The New Ager believes that God's plan, as he understands it, could be described in many Biblical references if the ''correct'' interpretation were placed on those references; and that the future is probably very similar to that presented above. But before the particulars of this plan can be understood, several articles of the New Ager's faith will have to be described in a relatively simple way. These Articles of Faith will be addressed in greater detail in subsequent chapters, particularly Chapter 6.

As Articles of Faith, the New Ager believes in several things. First, he believes that the populated earth is not unique in the universe, but that other populations and other worlds do exist. However, some of those other worlds may vibrate at multi-dimensional frequencies which can be detected solely as energy and light by mankind's existing five senses. Thus, a three-dimensional human would see these worlds only as aspects of energy and light. They would remain undetected as being other entities or worlds. Secondly, he believes that the earth has been locked into a restricting three-dimensional frequency warp for quite some time; however that many of earth's inhabitants have been able to overcome the three-dimensional restrictions by the efforts resulting from their Belief and Faith, and have ascended into a multi-dimensional existence. Thirdly, he believes that the entire Earth recently has been welcomed back into the company of the sacred planets and will join them soon by ascending into a multi-dimensional existence with them. And fourthly, he believes that a loving God would not leave unascended people on an ascended planet. To do so would be to leave them in an infernal world--the frequencies would be so far over their head that they would feel surrounded solely by energy and light. And so, as a part of His plan, He will give them additional chances to ascend.

Having said all of that, some New Agers believe that God's plan has recently been changed from previous plans because of mankind's growth and ability to evolve faster than expected, and now is as follows:

1. Instead of placing those who are on the Way in a safe place while the Earth undergoes cleansing and becomes capable of ascension, He will remove those who are not on the Way to another place similar to what Earth has been like for quite some time. In this place, they will be as comfortable as they have been on Earth. There they again can try to find the Way;

2. When those who cannot ascend at this time are safely out of the way, those who can ascend will do so in conjunction with an ascending planet [the New Earth] and in company with those who are also on the Way;

3. When ascended, the planet and people will be a part of that which is described in the Bible as the New Jerusalem; and

4. Although the time of the final ascension is as unknown to the New Ager as the Second Coming is to the Christian, it is believed that the first step of the plan will happen soon.

This plan, and how it has been changed from previous plans, is part of a constant study being conducted by those of the New Age. Its further investigation is beyond the scope of this particular study; but can be examined in many other New Age books.

SUMMARY

Both the Christian and the New Ager believe in a God who has some sort of a name, who is difficult to define, who has functional responsibilities which may or may not be similar, and who establishes a relationship with and has a plan for His people. In addition, just as Christians were defined as "belonging to the Way" in their early days, the New Ager has been described in a similar manner today. Finally, the New Ager believes that God has a plan which is eminent--somewhat as Christians have been believing for about 2,000 years.

In respect to thoughts about God, there is a great deal of similarity between the New Ager of today and the Christian of about 50 A.D., for the journey which the Christian has been making for the past 2,000 years or so seems to be somewhat like the journey the New Ager is starting on today. Today, just as then, there is much to explore, to learn, to develop and to make mistakes about. Hopefully the New Agers will not develop their own Crusades, or Inquisitions, or Salem Witch Trials, or Victorian Repressions all in the name of their God; although some activities similar to these have already occurred. As all will state, the New Age cultic activity which led to the massacre of some 912 people in the People's Temple of Jonestown, Guyana was a horror in the same league as the Christian-instigated stake-burning in England during the sixteenth century; and the mind-control cults of the New Age are abominations in the same order as the Spanish Inquisition of the fifteenth century. Hopefully, such activities will diminish to the point that they no longer will occur. Possibly the concerned and dedicated New Ager will be able to make this to happen and to establish his belief in God more fully, more expeditiously and less painfully than otherwise would be possible, if he would thoroughly examine the entire history of his Judeo-Christian-New Age heri-

"In those days Jesus came from Nazareth of Galilee and was baptized by John in the Jordan. And when he came up out of the water, immediately he saw the heavens opened and the Spirit descending upon him like a dove; and a voice came from heaven, 'Thou art my beloved Son; with thee I am well pleased.' "

The Bible, The Gospel According to Mark, 1:9-11

"And Jesus said, I cannot show the king, unless you see with eyes of soul, because the kingdom of the king is in the soul. And every soul a kingdom is. There is a king for every man. This king is love, and when this love becomes the greatest power in life, it is the Christ; so Christ is king. And every one may have this Christ dwell in his soul, as Christ dwells in my soul.

The Aquarian Gospel of Jesus the Christ, Chapter 71:4-7

"For yes, the Shepherd Jesus speaks to His sheep. He tells us of the universe to come and how the Higher Evolution will come to collect the faithful when the heavens are fully opened and all signs have been fulfilled."

The Keys of Enoch, Key 3-0-7:88

CHAPTER 3   JESUS CHRIST-- WHO, WHERE, WHAT AND WHY

The central figure of Christianity is, of course, Jesus Christ. The first part of this chapter will depict the life, the teachings and death of Jesus Christ as presented in the Scriptures and as believed in by the Christian; and the second part will describe the relevance of those same subjects to the beliefs of the New Ager.

THE LIFE OF CHRIST

GOSPELS   The life of Jesus the Christ is presented in the four Gospels of the New Testament of the holy Bible: the Gospels of Matthew, Mark, Luke and John. The word ''Gospel'' comes from the Old English word ''godspell'' which means ''good news'' and which was, itself, derived from the Latin word *evangelium*. Therefore, the four Gospel writers were presenting the ''good news of the coming of the Messiah''. Most Biblical scholars believe that Mark was written first, some time between AD 60 and 70; and that both Matthew and Luke used Mark as an outline for their longer Gospels. These three Gospels constitute the synoptic, or summary Gospels; whereas John, probably the last written, is considered to be more of a theological interpretation of the historical stories presented in the synoptic Gospels. None of the Gospels has been accurately dated, and the factual identity of the authors is still considered to be in doubt. Furthermore, the historical accuracy of the writings has been questioned by many scholars. However, most Christian scholars and believers accept the Gospels as being an accurate account of the life and times of Jesus Christ.

BIRTH   Matthew and Luke tell of the birth of Jesus; whereas neither Mark nor John do. Mark starts his Gospel with the baptism of Jesus; and John, after a short introductory hymn stating that He had been in existence since the beginning of time, also starts his story with the baptism of Jesus. The letters of Paul, many of which were written before the Gospels were written, also say nothing about the birth of Jesus, although the meaning of the life, the death and the Resurrection of Jesus Christ are constant themes in Paul's writings.

The birth of Jesus has created a lot of controversy within the Christian community. People of all religions have wanted their God to be different than they are, especially when He visits them on Earth; and that difference is often captured by the stories of His birth. The birth of Jesus as told by Matthew and Luke represents a fulfillment of the Old Testament prophecies, particularly that prophecy presented in Isaiah 7:14 which says: "Therefore the Lord himself will give you a sign. Behold, a young woman [or virgin] shall conceive and bear a son, and shall call his name Immanuel [which means 'God is with us']."

The birthplace of Jesus is reported to be Bethlehem of Judea, and although the date of the birth is unknown, it most probably was some time in the Spring of 5-7 B.C. After the establishment of Christianity as a religion, a body of the Faithful developed a tremendous amount of lore about the birth of Christ and the coincidental circumstances applicable to His mother, Mary. Although all Christians accept the circumstances of his life, death and Resurrection, not all accept the lore of his birth or the subsequent enhancement of that event which has been developed by man through the years.

BAPTISM   All of the Gospels tell of the baptism of Jesus, and that is where all Christians will accept the start of his ministry. The baptism of Jesus was an important event, for at that anointment, "behold, the heavens were opened and he saw the Spirit of God descending like a dove, and alighting on him; and lo, a voice from heaven saying, 'This is my beloved Son, with whom I am well pleased' " [Matthew 3:16-17]. The word "Christ" comes from the Greek word "Khristos" meaning "the Anointed One"; just as the word "Messiah" comes from similar Aramaic or Hebrew words which also mean "the Anointed One". Therefore, whether one says Jesus the Christ or Jesus the Messiah, he is saying the same thing: *viz.* that this Jesus whom Christians follow is the Anointed One, the Christ or the Messiah. And it also is understandable how the more formal term "Jesus the Christ" can become shortened to the more familiar term "Jesus Christ". By either title, Christians recognize Jesus as the Anointed One. The anointment certainly occurred at his baptism, if not before.

TEMPTATIONS   Following the baptism, the Gospels of Matthew and Luke report the Temptations of Christ. This is the first episode which highlights how Christ will conduct his ministry, for in this seminal event we see that Christ will get his priorities right as God's promised deliverer. In each Temptation, he demonstrated that he would not seek short-term solutions to long-term problems. Instead, he accepted suffering and humble service which he knew to be God's will. The Temptations demonstrate his complete acceptance of this fate.

The first Temptation was that of bringing on a new society

by economic means. As described in Luke 4:3-4, Jesus could have done this by turning stones into bread. Jesus was hungry, but then so was the whole world. Why not make a new economic order in which work and want would disappear, especially since this would fulfill Old Testament prophecy given by Isaiah and Ezekiel. There were plenty of reasons for Jesus to be concerned with economic matters such as food, shelter and clothing; but fame and the popularity of being an economic miracle worker did not represent the suffering and service which Jesus knew was his destiny. He therefore used Old Testament Scripture to help overcome the temptation to be only a breadwinner, even if he were to be the breadwinner for the entire world; for as stated in Deuteronomy 8:3, ''And he humbled you...that he might make you know that man does not live by bread alone, but that man lives by everything that proceeds out of the mouth of the Lord''. Jesus knew that people had economic needs, but their deeper need was an understanding of God. This was his main work. Later, he did provide food for the hungry through the miracle of the fishes and loaves; but this was only as an aid to his teaching. Jesus had a non-economic purpose for his life. He resisted the Temptation for his followers to have economic well-being without effort. And he later emphasized that to get rewards without effort was not his way He did this in the parable of the Talents [Matthew 25:14-30]. It is still a fact of economic life that rewards are not given without effort. In fact they are not worth having unless they are the result of effort. That is Christian. That is an eternal truth, whatever some people may say or think.

The second Temptation was that of showing how special he was. As described in Luke 4:9-13, he could do this by throwing himself down from a high temple into a crowded courtyard without hurting himself or anyone else. Now it would have been very easy for Jesus to show that he was the Promised One by doing such tricks, especially since Judaism had always appreciated tricks such as that. As an example, after the miracle of the loaves and the fishes, the crowd so loved his tricks that they wanted to make him King [John 6:15]. And so, it must have been a very appealing thought to give the crowd exactly what they wanted, especially since this would have fulfilled the prophecy of Malachi and particularly Psalm 91 which promises God's protection for those who were put to the test. But in Deuteronomy 6:16, those of the Judeo-Christian heritage are admonished not to put God to the test; and a careful reading and understanding of Psalm 91 shows that God's protection is available only to those who live in obedient service to God's will. For Jesus to do God's will, he had to undergo service and suffering, not to use God's promises for a selfish end. And so, Jesus again kept his priorities straight by resisting the temptation to be known as God's promised one merely by a display of miraculous power. He did perform miracles, but only as a sign of his message-- not as the message itself. And this is still true. God's miracles are only presented when they are a part of doing God's will.

The third Temptation was that of becoming a political Messiah. This had to be the strongest of all Temptations, for God had promised His people their own land; but for almost 600 years that had not happened. The Jews fully expected their Messiah to be a political Messiah who would lead them in their rule over other nations--almost like a Hitler or a Saddam Hussein. It must have been a great Temptation to accept Satan's worldly power in order to give a down-trodden people world leadership. How great to overthrow the tyranny of Rome's rule! How great not to have to pay taxes to Rome! How truly great to have Rome pay taxes to you! Jesus resisted this Temptation for two reasons: [1] he would have had to accept Satan as his Lord [Matt 4:8-10] whereas Jesus had just been baptized as accepting God; and [2] ruling an empire such as Rome was not his job, because God's rule in men's lives could never be imposed from the outside like all governments do. Instead of rules and regulations such as those promulgated by govern- ments, men needed to give their will and obedience to God and thus be given the moral freedom to create the kind of new society desired by God. Instead of an earthly kingdom of tyranny and cruelty by Jews to replace the similar authoritarianism of Rome, God's new society would be based on the inner nature of those who were a part of it as they served and worshipped God alone. And so, this most tempting of Temptations was rejected in the strongest of terms, "BEGONE SATAN!" This is still God's will today.

By the way he handled the Temptations, Jesus demonstrated conclusively how his ministry would be conducted and how Christianity would be practiced. There would be no short-term solutions to long-term problems. Christ would take his time, and do it right. He would live his life as directed by God; not as proposed by Satan.

FOLLOWERS   After the Temptations, Jesus started his ministry. Most of this ministry was spent as a religious teacher. It probably was an itinerate life as he wandered from place to place followed by his disciples. These disciples were picked by Jesus so that he would have someone capable of carrying on his work when he was not available. The choice of his disciples was an important part of the life of Jesus and he obviously chose well; for if he had not chosen capable followers as his disciples, there would probably be no Christians today. In fact, it is highly likely that no one would have ever heard the word "Christian" if it had not been for the activities of Christ's followers. Therefore, he must have chosen his followers well.

What do the Gospels tell us about these men that he chose? In Matthew, we see that Peter, Andrew, James and John were fishermen [4:18-22]; that Matthew [or Levi] was a tax collector and sinner [9:9]; and that finally there were 12 disciples whose names are not given [10:1]. In Mark, we are given the names of the same five as mentioned by Matthew, then in Mark 3:13, we are given the names of all twelve of the disciples. In Luke, we note the gathering of Levi, and then in 6:12-16, we are given the names of the twelve. In John, we see the gathering of the first five, then are presented with the chosen 12 without giving names [6:66-71].

And that is all that is given about the twelve disciples before they became disciples. Thus, very little is known about the early life of these people who were to become so important to the development of Christianity. However, it is highly likely that:

1. Twelve were chosen to give a symbolic relationship to the twelve tribes of Israel-Judea;

2. The latter seven, about whom almost nothing is known were probably plain people of all types and descriptions just like the identified five were; and

3. Jesus probably chose the twelve of them from among all of his followers because they had displayed some special trait or characteristic to him.

But the major point to be made is this: the disciples did not include a single notable such as Pontius Pilate, or Herod, or a leader of the Roman Legion, or anyone else with an outstanding track record or resume. They were just plain folk. And in his physical lifetime, Jesus did not select the well-educated Pharisee Saul, who later became Paul. In his lifetime, Jesus was not a mover and shaker and neither were his followers. And yet, his followers believed in him, followed his leadership, and could do his work when he wasn't around. The end result was that the world was moved and shaken as it never had been before.

NAMES   Who was Jesus? What did he call himself? During his lifetime he was known as a teacher or rabbi who taught in the synagogue or wherever he might meet people. Quite often this was out in the open countryside where the larger crowds could gather to hear him. It was as a teacher that Jesus caught the attention of the people, for it was obvious that this was no ordinary rabbi. He was not merely passing on what he had heard from others; he was teaching totally new things about men and women and their relationship with God. And he was saying them in such a way that no one could escape making a decision about what he was saying or about who he was. One either had to accept that he taught as one having authority, or to accept that he was the worst kind of religious fanatic. The teaching which caused this dichotomy was on just two subjects: [1] that Jesus was the promised deliverer whom the Jews were expecting; and [2] that the nature and meaning of the new society which Jesus came to inaugurate was to be different than anything which the Hebrew people had expected.

The Hebrew people had been looking for God to send them a Messiah. This Messiah would inaugurate a new society in which the Hebrew people would take the leadership role. With all the importance placed on that probability, it is somewhat disturbing to note that the word Messiah [or its Greek translation, Christ] is used so rarely in the Gospels. In Mark, the word is used only six times, only three of which refer to Jesus and only one in which Jesus refers to himself. Instead, Jesus identifies the Messiah with someone whom he calls "the Son of Man", an important concept which is used fourteen times in Mark and thirty-one times in Matthew. In fact, Jesus often uses this term to name himself, sometimes in an unclear manner. In some cases he simply uses it instead of saying "I" thus implying his human nature. At other times, he uses it to refer to the future when he will sit on the Right Hand of God. But most often he seems to use it to refer to the suffering and death that he would be going through. The term "Son of man" is used in reference to death and suffering almost three-fourths of the time. In this sense it presents a startling new concept--the thought of a God suffering in order to make life better for humans which, of course, is just the opposite of all previous God-Human relationships. It sets a process in which God can serve mankind rather than the reverse. This is truly a revolutionary and astounding concept!

During his lifetime, Jesus called himself four things: [1] the Son of Man; [2] the Messiah; [3] the Son of God; and [4] Servant.

68

All four are filled with meaning for there is no doubt that by using them, Jesus is claiming a unique relationship with God, and a unique authority. As the Son of Man, he would suffer to fulfill God's plan; as the Messiah, he would fulfill the promises of God's prophets albeit in an unexpected way; as the Son of God, he would have a special relationship with God; and as Servant, he would create a new relationship between God and mankind.

SUMMARY   During his lifetime, Jesus demonstrated superb leadership qualities in at least three major ways:

1 He did not accept short-term solutions to long-term problems. In other words, he kept his priorities straight by resisting the temptations which would have diverted him from the priorities established by God;

2. He gave no recognition of status when choosing his followers, but found people who believed in him, followed his leadership and had the talent do his work when he was absent; and

3 He described himself as the Son of Man who suffered, as the Son of God who had a special relationship with God, and as a Servant, primarily by his activities. He never said that he was the Messiah until after he had already been convicted of being that, but then he accepted the role when it became obvious that others had recognized him as such.

Because of the life he led which demonstrated these and other qualities, Christians accept their Lord as one who was a great leader by anyone's standard, and as a teacher who taught the people of the world how to live--if they would just do it! Christians believe that his was the greatest life that was ever lived.

THE TEACHINGS OF CHRIST

During his ministry on Earth, Jesus Christ was a Teacher who taught the people of the world how to live--if they would just do it. In order for Christians to learn how to live, most feel that they need to understand the teachings of Christ as represented by his sermons, his parables, and his examples. The development of such an understanding would require a tremendous input of time--a lifetime or more. Consequently, the following will merely scratch the surface.

SERMONS   The Scriptures record only one sermon by Jesus Christ, ''The Sermon on the Mount'' [Matthew 5:1-48]. It is unlikely that this sermon was given all at once, but probably is a compendium of a number of sermons. It is also unlikely that Jesus Christ gave only one sermon. He probably preached quite often. But the one recorded sermon is a superb example of his teaching. The Sermon on the Mount is not law. Instead it is a poetic presentation of a set of principles by which a life should be lived. Such principles are rarely effective when enacted as law, since most laws are based on calculations of how people can be expected to behave. Since a law that would not be kept or could not be enforced would tend to put pressure on people to become what they are not, it would be a bad law. But this is exactly what Jesus' teaching does. In particular, the principles in the Sermon on the Mount teach Christians to become different than they naturally or normally would be. Because of this, it is good teaching.

Because the Sermon on the Mount presented the followers of Christ with principles for guiding their life rather than laws which must be rigorously obeyed and enforced, it created quite a conflict with the Pharisees who wanted a law to govern every possible act. Rather than enforceable law, the Sermon on the Mount presented unenforceable principles. In this manner, the

70

Sermon is much like an article entitled ''Law and Manners'' which was presented in 1924 by Lord Moulton, and which states:

''In order to explain this extraordinary title, I must ask you to follow me in examining the three great domains of Human Action. First comes the domain of POSITIVE LAW, where our actions are prescribed by laws binding upon us which must be obeyed. Next comes the domain of FREE CHOICE, which includes all those actions as to which we claim and enjoy complete freedom. But between these two, there is a third and important domain in which there rules neither POSITIVE LAW nor ABSOLUTE FREEDOM. In that domain there is no law which inexorably determines our course of action, and yet we feel that we are not free to choose as we would. The degree of this sense of a lack of complete freedom in this domain varies in every case. It grades from a consciousness of Duty nearly as strong as POSITIVE LAW, to a feeling that it is all but a question of personal choice.

''Some might wish to parcel out this domain into separate countries...but I prefer to look at it as all one domain, for it has one and the same characteristic throughout--it is the domain of **Obedience** to the **Unenforceable**. The obedience is the obedience of a man to that which he cannot be forced to obey. He is the enforcer of the law upon himself.

'' This country which lies between Law and Free Choice I always think of as the domain of MANNERS. To me, Manners in this broad sense signifies the doing that which you should do although you are not obliged to do it. ...It covers all cases of right doing where there is no one to make you do it but yourself.''

Lord Moulton went on to say that the true test of greatness of a nation rests in the ''extent to which the individuals composing the nation can be trusted to obey self-imposed law.''[8]

There is a parallel between the Sermon on the mount and Lord Moulton's speech in that the sermon by Jesus becomes the

Lord Moulton's speech in that the sermon by Jesus becomes the guiding principles for living which the Christian imposes upon himself. The Sermon on the Mount presents the Christian with teaching about how to live his life--if he would just do it!

PARABLES   At least two-thirds of the teachings of Jesus are recorded as Parables. There are 22 Parables presented in the synoptic Gospels, some of which are presented in all three. In addition, some of the ''I am'' sayings in the Gospel of John are similar to the parables of the synoptic Gospels.

A Parable has three characteristics: [1] it is Eastern in philosophy in that the questioner must answer the question for himself; [2] it represents an enigma in that there are different answers for different people; and [3] it is like an onion in that it has many layers of understanding. Once one of the lessons in a parable is understood, then another lesson will be discovered underneath it. Parables, therefore, represent teaching which is subject to a lot of interpretation and understanding on the part of the learner. This initially confused the disciples as described in Matthew 13; 10-14 which says:
''Then the disciples came and said to him, 'Why do you speak to them in parables?' And he answered them, 'To you it has been given to know the secrets of the kingdom of heaven, but to them it has not been given. For to him who has will more be given, and he will have abundance; but from him who has not, even what he has will be taken away. This is why I speak to them in parables, because seeing they do not see, and hearing they do not hear, nor do they understand....' ''

But to the Christian who understands, the Parables present a wealth of information related to the life they should live.

EXAMPLES   Possibly the most meaningful teaching done by Jesus Christ during his ministry on Earth was his teaching by example. Some of these examples were human in nature while others were beyond the normal human experience. As three examples of human experience, Jesus Christ dined with sinners [Matt. 9:10]; he showed love to the Samaritans [John 4:9]; and he washed the feet of his disciples [John 13:5]. None of these activities would have been done by a right-thinking person of the Hebrew faith. By these and other human examples, Jesus Christ taught his followers how to live differently than they had.

Jesus Christ also taught by examples which were beyond normal human experiences. These were the miracles performed by Jesus. There are eighteen acts reported in the Gospels which are accepted as miracles by Christian scholars. Many of these acts are related to healing. And by these examples, Jesus taught his followers what was possible for them to do, for he also said, "Truly, truly I say to you, he who believes in me will also do the works that I do; and greater works than these will he do because I go to the Father." [John 14:12]. By these and other examples, Jesus Christ taught his followers what they could do with their lives.

SUMMARY   Jesus Christ was a great teacher. This fact is admitted to even by those who do not accept him as their personal Lord and Savior, for Jesus Christ is honored as a great teacher by those who are of the Islamic, the Buddhist, the Shinto and many other Faiths. But to the Christian, great as Jesus Christ is as a teacher, he is much, much more than merely that.

THE CONFLICTS CREATED BY CHRIST

The teachings of Jesus Christ created conflicts with the practices of many of the existing elements of the Jewish society. As one example, the sermons and the parables of Christ created a significant conflict with the Pharisees because Christ was preach-

principles rather than by the letter of the law. But other examples are available to show that Christ created conflicts with more than just the Pharisees. He created significant conflicts with at least three influential religious groups and three influential political groups or people. They are: the Pharisees, the Sadducees, the Essenes, the Zealots, Herod Antipas and Pontius Pilate.

BACKGROUND To understand these conflicts and the inevitable result of such conflict creation, interested Christians should understand something about the nature of these groups by examining their beliefs and their status during the time of Jesus' ministry.

PHARISEES The Pharisees were laymen, not priests. They were the forerunners of the present-day Rabbis or teachers. In Jesus' time, they served the present day Rabbi function as teachers of and interpreters of the Law. They were very serious about understanding, teaching, keeping, and interpreting the religious laws, including all oral interpretations. The Law was a very important and complex part of the Hebrew society of two thousand years ago. The basis of this Law was found in the Torah, also known as the Pentateuch, which consists of the first five books of the present-day Old Testament. The Law started with the Ten Commandments [Exodus 34] but went much further than just that. In Exodus, the Ten Commandments are followed by at least 38 ordinances, and there are many, many more ordinances presented in Deuteronomy. By the time of Christ, the laws and their interpretations had expanded to encompass almost every facet of Hebrew religious and secular life. The Pharisees had the job of telling people what the Law said that they could do, and even seeing that they did it. The Pharisees had a position of great power within their society, because they sat on Moses' seat in the Synagogue with full authority to interpret the Scriptures. They covered the entire political spectrum, but were generally conservative in their theological activities. They had a great influence on the people and were known as the ''Friends of the People'' in contrast to the priestly Sadducees or the aloof Essenes. They were the largest group in the Hebrew religious community They were well entrenched, liked their work and felt that they were doing God's will as they understood it. In one word, they could be described as the ''Respected''.

SADDUCEES   The Sadducees were the priestly families, mostly living in Jerusalem or in Jericho. They were descendants of Zadok who had anointed Solomon. Their position was generally an inherited one. They were the aristocratic, wealthy, ''old-line'' families who assimilated the Greek and Roman cultures. They believed God would reward Good with wealth and health, and would punish Evil with sickness and poverty. They did not believe in Heaven, Hell, resurrection or an afterlife of any form. They cooperated with the Romans in order to preserve worship in the Temple as directed by themselves. They controlled the ruling Sanhedrin during Jesus' time. The Sanhedrin was the highest judicial and ecclesiastical council of the ancient Hebrew nation, composed of about 70 members, some two-thirds of whom were from the Sadducees. Their main concern was Temple Worship. In one word, they could be described as the ''Ins''.

ESSENES   Though they are not mentioned in the Bible, the Essenes were the second largest religious group in Jesus' time. They were scattered in Communities throughout the Judean wilderness. They are described in the Dead Sea Scrolls and other such findings. At the time of Jesus, they were very active. They believed the Temple priests to be illegitimate and the Temple to be corrupt. They were rigid and conservative in their belief. They did not marry and they remainded celibate. They had no children except for those who were adopted into the Community. They prayed for the Messiah to come, and believed that the end of the world would come within their lifetime at which time their Communities and their leadership in Heaven would be exactly as it had been on Earth, with their Earthly Leader becoming their Heavenly Leader. In one word, they could be described as the "Outs".

ZEALOTS   The Zealots were more political than religious in their activities. They violently opposed the Roman rule and occupation. They were eager for revolt and prayed constantly for a Messiah-King who would lead the uprising. The Zealots consisted of ex-slaves, super-patriots and even some bandits. It is thought that one of Jesus' disciples, the man called Simon, was a Zealot. It is also believed that Judas Iscariot and Barrabas, whom the crowd chose to liberate instead of Jesus, were also Zealots, but none of this is recorded in the Scriptures. The Zealots had four beliefs: [1] that they would serve no one except God; [2] that they opposed slavery; [3] that they preferred death, even by suicide, to slavery; and [4] that they violently opposed Rome by refusing to pay taxes or cooperating in any way with the Hebrew or Roman authorities. They were thought to hide a sword in their bed to be ready to take up arms for the Messiah when he came. They were willing to die for their cause. They were close in their religious beliefs to the Pharisees, but they were extremists. In one word, they could be described as the "Rebels".

HEROD ANTIPAS   Herod Antipas was the Herod who ruled during the time of John the Baptist and Jesus. He was one of the three surviving sons of Herod the Great who had ruled when Jesus was born and who, according to Matthew but to no other biblical record, had the children of Bethlehem murdered just as he had, by historical record, murdered one of his own sons who had attempted to succeed him. Herod the Great ruled from 37 BC to his death in 4 BC. All of the Herods were part Jewish, and thus Rome thought that they would be acceptable to the people as rulers. When Herod the Great died, Rome divided his Kingdom among the three surviving sons. Herod Antipas was given the northern portion which included Galilee. He was a crafty man who lived in luxury and built great buildings. He was the Herod who beheaded John the

Baptist, and who was still ruling a part of the Kingdom at the time of Jesus' trial.

PONTIUS PILATE   In 6 AD, Judea was reclassified by Rome. Instead of being a protectorate, it became a third-grade province. It therefore was to be ruled by a Roman procurator who reported to the Roman governor of Syria. Thus, Archelaus, another of Herod the Great's sons was kicked out of office and replaced by a Roman. The procurator of Judea who is best known to us is Pontius Pilate, a Roman who ruled from AD 26 to 36. He was procurator at the time of Jesus' trial.

CONFLICTS With this background, the interested Christian can better understand how Jesus created conflict with these groups; for he certainly did create conflicts with all of them.

PHARISEES   The Pharisees wanted to keep the Law. In addition, they wanted to avoid all sinners. Finally, they had worked for several centuries to convert the old tribal laws of retribution into a kinder and more gentle set of laws which demanded an "eye for an eye or a tooth for a tooth", rather than "a life for any insult". They were proud of such progress, and they were proud of the position in society which they had achieved. But Jesus created conflicts with all that the Pharisees wanted to do. In respect to the Law, he said that he had come to fulfill the Law [Matt 5:17]. In respect to sinners, he dined with them [Matt. 9:10]. In respect to the law of retribution, he said that you should forgive and not seek any retribution [Matt. 5:38-9]. And as a final act of defiance Jesus repeatedly said "Woe to you, scribes and Pharisees, hypocrites!" [Matthew Chapter 23]. Jesus threw cold water on everything that the Pharisees had been doing for centuries. He completely rejected them and their activities. In almost everything that he did, he created conflict with the Pharisees. As a result, they forced him into a trial, first by the Hebrew authorities and later by the Romans.

SADDUCEES   The Sadducees wanted to preserve Temple Worship and their position in it. They also had recently denied the space previously reserved for worship by the Gentiles in the Temple by throwing the Gentiles out and turning their space over to the bankers and money-changers. This made Jesus so angry that he threw those who bought and sold out of the Temple [Mark 11:15] and even predicted that the Temple would be torn down [Luke 21:5-6]. These acts angered and frightened the Sadducees for whom the Temple was everything. In addition, when Jesus claimed to be the Messiah, the Sadducees who supported Rome in order to keep their own authority over the Temple became concerned about their position in the world. If Christ were the Messiah, then where did they fit in? They felt that their authority was being threatened, an ultimate form of conflict creation. As a result of these conflicts, the Sadducees ardently supported the trial of Jesus.

ESSENES   The Essenes had less conflict with Jesus than did any other major religious group, and as a consequence, had less to do with the trial of Jesus and the causing of his death. However, they did not support Jesus when he went to Jerusalem. As a consequence, they had an indirect hand in his trial and execution. Why did they not support him? Possibly because Jesus taught in the Temple whereas the Essenes rejected anything concerning the Temple; and also possibly because Jesus was fun-loving and out-going whereas the Essenes were dour and rigid. In any event, the Essenes were not comfortable with him, not only because of his personality, but also because he did not preach the immediacy of the end of the world; whereas that was one of the major reasons for the existence of the Essenes. Because of these conflicts, the Essenes did not come to the support of Jesus at the time of his trial.

ZEALOTS   The Zealots could not accept Jesus because although he came as the Messiah, he came without the political uprising which the Zealots demanded. Also, Jesus advised paying taxes to

Rome when he advised the Pharisees to "Render therefore to Caesar the things that are Caesar's" [Matt. 22:21]. As a result, he was supporting the worldly rule of Rome rather than overturning it. This is exactly the opposite of what the Zealots wanted. Again, Jesus was throwing cold water on someone's most precious dream. As a result, the Zealots gave Jesus absolutely no support at the time of his trial.

HEROD ANTIPAS   Herod Antipas feared John the Baptist for a number of reasons, but principally because he was afraid that the people would instigate a political revolt based on their belief that John was a prophet [Matt. 14:1-12]. Consequently, he had John arrested and later beheaded. He also had similar feelings about Jesus, for, after all, Jesus had attracted even larger crowds than had John; and at one time a crowd of some 5,000 had wanted Jesus to become their King [John 6:1-15]. Because of his popularity, Jesus was feared by Herod Antipas, the highest ranking non-Roman authority in the country. Fear and conflict-creation are often related.

PONTIUS PILATE   Pontius Pilate was the Roman authority who had the power to carry out the Roman laws whereas the Sanhedrin did not. One of the Roman laws which was at the disposal of Pilate was the crucifixion of those who had committed a treasonous act against Rome. One such act could be a person declaring himself to be king. And so, after Jesus had been put on trial, first in the house of Annas before daylight, and then at the Sanhedrin after daylight when they could meet, the priests and elders took him to Pilate [John 18-19]. At first, they wanted Pilate to condemn Jesus to death merely on their say-so; but when Pilate refused, they stated that Jesus had declared himself King and thus had committed treason. When Pilate questioned Jesus, he realized that the kingship in question was not that of Rome, but merely represented a conflict between those of the Hebrew Faith. And so, again Pilate refused to condemn Jesus. When the Hebrew authorities realized that their religious conflicts had no effect on Pilate, they then accused Jesus of perverting the Hebrew nation and of refusing to pay taxes to Rome. Although Pilate continued to believe that Jesus was not guilty of any crime under Roman law, he did accept the fact that Jesus had upset the Hebrew leadership. Consequently, Pilate was caught in a trap. He knew that if he freed Jesus, he would face a riot; but if he condemned Jesus, he would have to live with a guilty conscience for the rest of his life. Pilate tried one more dodge. He tried to release Jesus on the custom of releasing one condemned man at the Passover, but the Hebrew priests and elders chose Barabbas instead. Pilate then feared that the crowds were getting ready to riot, and it was this fear which finally forced his hand. He simply did not want any bad reports of his conduct going back to Rome and so he refused to free Jesus. And this was the only conflict which Jesus forced on Pilate--that of a man fearing a bad report going to his superiors. On this fear alone, Pilate delivered Jesus to his accusers.

RESULT OF THE CONFLICTS Jesus created conflict with many of the major elements of the Hebrew society of his day: *viz.* with the Pharisees, the Sadducees, the Essenes, the Zealots, the Jewish and the Roman rulers. The result of these conflicts is very simple. They crucified him. As was usual, they hung a placard on his chest to state the offence. It said, ''Jesus of Nazareth, the King of the Jews''. This fact is recorded on both the Roman and the Jewish histories of the time in addition to being presented in the Gospels. In those histories it is stated that the one called ''The King of the Jews'' had been crucified during the procuratorship of Pontius Pilate.

Nicholi Machiavelli [1469-1527] was a political leader in Renaissance Florence. He wrote a book entitled The Prince. It is still considered to be a masterpiece of political literature. In that book, Machiavelli says: ''There is nothing more difficult to take in hand, more perilous in its conduct, or more uncertain of success as to take the lead in the introduction of a new order of things''. Jesus Christ took the lead in the introduction of a new order of things. It was an undertaking which was difficult, perilous, and uncertain of success. It caused him to be crucified; but in the mind of the Christian, the leader who introduced the new order of things was a complete success.

THE EFFECTS OF THE CRUCIFIXION AND RESURRECTION OF JESUS CHRIST

As he says when he recites the Apostles' Creed, the practicing Christian believes that Jesus Christ ''...was crucified, dead, and buried; the third day He rose again from the dead; he ascended into heaven, and sitteth on the right hand of God the Father Almighty; from thence He shall come to judge the quick and the dead...'' Although all the words of The Apostles' Creed are important, possibly the most important are the words ''rose again'' for without that having happened, nothing else would have mattered. The most important central issue to the faith of a Christian is his belief in the Resurrection of his Lord and Savior, Jesus Christ. There are several lasting effects of this Resurrection. One is Easter; another is the relevance of that seminal event to the Christian's belief; and a third is the establishment of the Christian Church.

EASTER   Good Friday is the day during which the Christian remembers the Crucifixion; and Easter is a day during which the Christian celebrates the Resurrection of Jesus Christ. Easter is the Christian's most important day. Without Easter there would be no Christmas, for there would be no need. Without Easter, there would be no Christians, for the movement would simply have folded up and disappeared. Easter is the reason for existence of Christianity. Consequently, to understand why he follows Christ, the Christian must understand Easter, particularly the fact that the Crucifixion and the Resurrection actually happened.

81

The Crucifixion happened. It is recorded in historical records other than the Bible. In both the history of the Jews as written by Josephus and in the history of the Roman Legions, there is a recording that during the procuratorship of Pontious Pilate in Jerusalem, the man known as the King of the Jews had been crucified by the Romans. Since there were thousands of crucifixions performed in Palestine during the rule of the Romans, if the crucifixion of Jesus Christ had not been recorded, then Christians could not have assumed that it did not occur; but since it is recorded, then Christians must assume that it not only happened, it made such an impression on both the Romans and the Jews that each recorded it as an historical fact in their separate histories of the time. If it had been in only one history but not the other, then Christians could worry about fraud or a later adjustment of the records to retroactively lead credence to the earthly death of Christ. But to accept such a doctoring of two separate histories stretches the imagination. By all logical arguments, the Crucifixion of Jesus Christ is an historical fact.

The Resurrection of Jesus Christ falls more into the area of Christian belief than into the area of historical fact as substantiated by non-Christian records. Nevertheless, the Christian bases his belief on three rather striking facts:
1. That those who were there were convinced that it did happen;
2. That the Resurrection was not prophesied in the Old Testament; and
3. That the Resurrection is accepted as fact by all believing Christians.

Any doubt that those who were there were convinced that it happened can be dispelled by merely reading the fifteenth Chapter of I Corinthians. This Letter from Paul to the Church at Corinth is one of the earlier writings of the New Testament. It was written in about 52 AD, some 10-25 years before the Gospels were written. Paul did not write this part of the Letter to convince anyone; he merely wrote it to remind everyone of that which they know to be true. It starts out with, "Now I would remind you..." and then goes on to state in unequivocal terms that Christ was raised from the dead and that the risen Christ had been seen by more than five hundred disciples, many of whom were still alive when he wrote this Letter and thus could confirm or challenge him [I Cor. 15:6]. Those who were there at the time never doubted it. They accepted it as a fact.

But possibly even more remarkable than the foregone conclusions presented in Paul's first Letter to the Corinthians is the indisputable fact that a thoroughly disheartened band of disciples, who should by all rules of historical probability have been depressed and disillusioned by their Master's Crucifixion were, in the space of seven short weeks, transformed into a strong band of courageous witnesses and the nucleus of a constantly growing church. The central fact of their witness was that Christ was alive and active, and they had no hesitation in attributing the change in themselves to what had happened as a result of his rising from the dead. They themselves were obviously convinced that this was what actually happened. The Resurrection was not something that they merely talked about; it was something that they were willing to die for. People don't do that unless they believe it to be true. And in the early days, to be an Apostolic preacher, you had to have seen the risen Christ. That was a requirement when the disciples searched for a replacement for Judas. Those who were there were convinced that it happened.[9]

In respect to the second striking fact, the Old Testament expresses a very negative attitude about the possibility of resurrection. In fact, the priestly Sadducees rejected it completely. Therefore, the Resurrection did not have to happen in order to fulfill Old Testament prophecies, because none of the prophecies about

83

Messiah refer to his resurrection in any way. The Resurrection is really a watershed from Old Testament to New Testament philosophy. Despite this lack of a need for the Resurrection to occur, an analysis of every early Christian message about Jesus Christ fits into the following outline:

1. Jesus has fulfilled the Old Testament promises and prophecies;
2. God was at work in His life, death and Resurrection;
3. Jesus has now been exalted to Heaven;
4. The Holy Spirit has been given to the Church;
5. Jesus will soon return in Glory; and
6. Men and women who hear the message must respond to its challenge.[10]

If the word "Resurrection" is removed from item 2 of the above outline, then none of what follows in the outline makes any sense. Almost the entire existence of the early church was based on the belief that Jesus was no longer dead, but was alive! Although not required to fulfill Old Testament prophecies, the Resurrection became an integral part of the New Testament. It is the single act which separates the New Testament from the Old.

As a consequence, any Christian who believes in the New Testament must believe in the Resurrection of Jesus Christ. Again, in I Corinthians, Paul has merely reminded those on-the-spot of something that they have always known and accepted--that Christ died and came back to life. Paul knew and accepted this, and writes about the acceptance of the Resurrection as being required of every Christian. Paul, the earliest recorded writer in the New Testament of the Bible, presents that requirement without ever mentioning the Virgin Birth. To Paul, Easter was everything, and Christmas was of no import.

RELEVANCE   The crucifixion and resurrection have relevance to both Old Testament and New Testament thinking and philosophy The first Old Testament relevance is found in the story of Abraham and his son, Isaac [Genesis 22:1-20]. In this story, God is testing the Faith of Abraham. He knows the great love that Abraham has for his son; but He also knows of the great love that Abraham has for Him. Which is greater? Will Abraham give up his only son in order to show his love for God? And so, the test is given. Abraham is not found lacking. He loves nothing more than God. He is willing to sacrifice his beloved son in order to do God's will. But then we see God's love in action. He tells Abraham that he doesn't have to sacrifice his son. And even today, God does not need us to express our love to Him in such a dramatic way. But on the other hand, God does want to show His love for us in exactly that way. He sacrificed His son to show His love for us. It happened during the Crucifixion. The Crucifixion Story and the Abraham Story have much in common. They must be understood together in order that the Christian might appreciate God's love; for as remembered on Good Friday, He would do for us what He does not require us to do for Him. That is true love.

The second Old Testament relevance is found in the story of the Passover [Exodus 12:1-28]. This is a story which takes some Christians a long time to understand, for if we define our God as being omniscient [all knowing], omnipotent [all powerful] and omnipresent [in all places], then it seems to be a pretty stupid God who would need a spot of lamb's blood on the doorpost or lintel in order to know if the boy sleeping inside was a Hebrew or an Egyptian boy. And how could an all-knowing God be so stupid? And why should the Passover be so important to the Judeo-Christian heritage anyway? Of course, the point is that God loves to test the Faith of His followers and to give them the responsibility for taking the first step. That is exactly what He is doing in the Passover Story in which the directions for saving yourself and your family are pretty specific. "Just do as I say and I will believe that you have Faith in Me", says God; or "Let Me know that you have the Faith, and I will be for you", says God. He said that to His

85

Chosen People prior to the Exodus, and He says that to all Christians today. He said it in Egypt by using the blood of the unblemished Lamb; He says it to Christians today by using the blood of the unblemished Christ. In the Exodus Story, God passed over the Chosen People and their sins. He did that because they showed that they had Faith in Him by obeying His directions however silly those directions may have seemed at the time to those who chose not to believe. Today, the Christian believes that God passes over his sins because he shows Faith in Him by believing in the Resurrection of His Son, Jesus Christ, however silly that may seem to those who choose not to believe. ''Accept Jesus Christ and Him crucified as your Savior, and I will be for you'', says the Christian's God. The parallel to the Passover Story in the Old Testament is quite striking.

There are also relevant meanings for the Crucifixion and the Resurrection in the New Testament. Some of the relevance is: [1] as an historical Battle which is as significant a watershed mark as Gettysburg or D-Day; [2] as a loving Example which is an expression of God's overpowering love for His followers; [3] as a Sacrifice to once and forever permit a reconciliation between God and His people if His followers were only to let it happen; [4] as a Ransom by which He paid the price instead of having His followers do it; [5] as a Substitute by which He died thus permitting the price to be paid by Him rather than by his followers. All of these have meaning. All help to define the relevance of the Crucifixion and the Resurrection. But to the involved Christian, the real relevance relates to forgiveness, for to that Christian, the Cross shows the price of God's forgiveness. To that Christian, the true relevance of the Crucifixion and the Resurrection is that he has been forgiven.

CHURCH   The Church of Christ became a world-wide religion because it was accepted as the state religion of Rome. From there it grew to all corners of the Earth. The beginnings of Rome's acceptance of Christianity occurred in 312 AD. In that year, Rome became so badly split that Diocletian abdicated as emperor. The two most likely successors were Constantine who was in the field in the West, and Maxentius who was in Rome. As often happens, the two contestants rounded up their loyal followers and prepared to come to battle. When Constantine approached Rome for the decisive battle, he found that he was greatly outnumbered by Maxentius. In addition, Maxentius had a strong defensive position and was supported by the Pretorian Guard who had always picked the winning side and had ultimately decided who should be Caesar. According to later testimony, on the 27th of October, 312, Constantine had a dream. He was shown a sign which was the combination of the Greek letters Chi and Rho. These are the first two letters of the name ''Christ'' in Greek. These letters had been adapted in monogram form by the persecuted Christians in Greece. In Constantine's dream, the Latin words, *''Hoc signo victoreris''* appeared beneath the Greek monogram. These words mean, ''By this sign you shall be victor''. At dawn, Constantine ordered the sign to be painted on every soldier's shield, and the soldiers were challenged with, ''By this sign, you will be victorious''. Against overwhelming odds and against a very strong defensive position, on the 28th of October, 312 AD, the soldiers of Constantine were victorious at one of the world's greatest battles, the Battle of Milvian Bridge. After the battle, Constantine accepted Christ, and forever after gave Christ credit for all of his triumphs.

For some background on Constantine, it is noted that he had been raised in what is now called Turkey until age 13 and while there, presumably spoke only Latin. From age 13 to 32, Constantine was constantly in the West where he neither spoke nor heard Greek. It is also a matter of note that Freud, and most other psychiatrists, believe that people dream only in the language in which they think. Therefore, it is virtually impossible to explain the dream of Constantine which consequently becomes one of those undefined mysteries of God.

By most standards, Constantine was hardly much of a Christian. But he did unify the church by calling the conference at Nicaea [in western Turkey] where he had a splendid summer palace. During this conference the Nicene Creed was developed, and Christ became more like a Roman God by losing a lot of His Jewish humanity. But Christianity survived Constantine, the Nicene Conference, the Crusades, the Inquisition, the Salem Witch Trials, the Victorian repression, and even the recent "God is Dead" movement. And today, Christians gather together in his name, and for his purpose. Christians believe that because of Christmas, Christ entered the world for a normal life span; but because of Easter, he is with the world forever. Christians believe in the Crucifixion and the Resurrection of Jesus Christ and accept the relevance and the consequences of that belief.

THE NEW AGE VIEWPOINT

The person and divinity of Jesus Christ is as important to many New Agers as it is to most Christians; but just as there are Christians to whom Jesus Christ is more or less important than he is to other Christians, there are New Agers to whom the same is true. It is probable that if a curve describing the importance of Jesus Christ to Christians were developed, it would be a rather narrow, bell-shaped curve skewed toward the side of "more important." The same curve would describe the feelings of the New Ager, but the curve would probably be flatter, broader and more centered. In other words, although many practicing Christians would feel that Christ was important in their lives and within New Age some would feel the same, in Christianity some have not dedicated their life to Christ, and the same would be true for many within New Age. However, most students of either religion would not deny either the person or the divinity of Jesus Christ.

Jesus Christ is the central figure of Christianity, and the previous Section tried to present how he might be viewed by a

Christian. This Section will attempt to describe the feelings of the New Ager on the same subject, using the outline and topics which were used in the prior Section.

In respect to THE LIFE OF CHRIST, the New Ager will have a spectrum of beliefs about the GOSPELS similar to that found in the Christian Church. In other words, within the New Age movement will be found those who will literally accept every word of the four Gospels, those who will individually interpret every word of the four Gospels as God guides them in their interpretation, and those who will be in between these two extremes, just as there is within Christianity. In addition, there will be people in the New Age movement who know virtually nothing about the Gospels, just as there is within Christianity. But as one difference, within the New Age movement there will probably be many more people who have read, studied and prayed about the Apocryphal Gospels than will normally be found within the Christian Church. The acceptance of Apocryphal study by the individual represents one major difference between the New Ager and the Christian. Some of that material has been used in the development of this book

New Agers will also have no problem with the spectrum of beliefs about the BIRTH of Jesus, since their beliefs cover as wide a range as those of the Christians. These beliefs range from not feeling the necessity of accepting a supernatural instead of a natural act for his creation, all the way to that of believing that neither Jesus nor Mary had a physical father. For those who need no supernatural act as an Article of Faith, some New Agers, like many Christians, understand that the only reference to a virgin birth in the Gospels is Matthew 1:22-23 which merely states that everything concerning the birth of Jesus came about to fulfill the prophecy of Isaiah. In Isaiah 7:14, in the King James Version of the Bible [published in 1611] the prophet says ''...Behold, a virgin shall conceive...''; whereas in the Revised Standard Version of the Bible [published in 1973], the prophet says ''...Behold, a young woman shall

89

conceive..." and merely footnotes the words "or virgin" in place of the words "young woman". Like many Christians, these New Agers feel that the choice of translation between "virgin" and "young woman" is too close or too arbitrary to base an Article of Faith on. And in addition, most New Agers, like many Christians, will note that in The Apostles' Creed, the part of that belief which says "...born of the Virgin Mary.." uses the capital letter "V" so that the term is more of a title than a description of the conceptual act. In this sense, it is used like the title "Maid Marian" in Robin Hood, which is much more of a title than a description of the sexual history of the woman. On the other hand, many New Agers accept the Edgar Cayce readings[11] which state that since Jesus and Mary were of the same soul from the beginning of creation, then neither of them had a physical father--a belief similar to that of the Roman Catholic and Eastern Orthodox Churches. But despite all of this reasoning, most New Agers, like many Christians, will not argue the point because they believe that the argument is a non-essential one. They believe that it is of utmost importance that Jesus came to Earth so that "God is with us"; but they do not think that how he came would have any impact on the fact of his divinity. In other words, they believe that the fact that he came is much more important than how he came. Furthermore, they believe that the method of his birth is not described in the scriptures as written in their original languages. This lack of biblical justification for the "virgin birth" is further discussed in great detail in Chapter Seven.

But as another subject which relates to the BIRTH issue, New Agers adore, venerate and sanctify Mary to an extent not found within any Christian church with the possible exception of the Roman Catholic or the Eastern Orthodox Churches. They believe that Mary has a strong role in the fulfillment of God's Plan as they understand it. They believe that this role is not effected, one way or the other, by any question relating to her physical state at the time of the conception of Jesus Christ.

The New Ager recognizes the BAPTISM of Jesus as a seminal event to an extent which is probably stronger than that expressed by most Christians. To the New Ager, the sacrament of baptism is an extremely important act for any entity, but particularly for an Ascended Master such as Jesus. This importance is described in detail in Chapter 4.

The earlier sections relating to the TEMPTATIONS or the FOLLOWERS could have been written by a New Ager or by a Christian. It is probable that little if any disagreement would develop between a typical Christian or a typical New Ager on any part of either section.

The section on NAMES presents the basis for a very important distinction between the beliefs of the typical New Ager and the beliefs of the typical Christian. The New Age beliefs are presented in greater detail in Chapters 5 and 6; and the differences between these beliefs and the beliefs of established Christianity are presented in great detail in Chapter 7. For the present, let it suffice to say that the New Ager believes that when Jesus called himself the Son of Man, he was stating that he was just like any human on Earth; and when he called himself the Son of God, he was stating that since he was capable of being both a Son of Man and a Son of God, then others can also be both. This distinction probably causes the greatest theological difference between the New Ager and the Christian, particularly the fundamental Christian. But just as literal Christian Apologetics have arguments that Jesus is the only Son of God as an Article of Christian Faith, New Age practitioners present Articles of Faith that do not deny that Jesus was a Son of God, for the New Ager does not deny the divinity of Jesus Christ, merely his exclusivity.

The New Ager would have no disagreement with the SUMMARY of THE LIFE OF CHRIST as presented earlier, but would submit that the scriptural presentation of his life and times is incomplete. As one example, the New Ager believes that Jesus spent a large portion of the years between about ages 12 and 30 in the Far East [India and Tibet], and that non-Biblical historical records substantiate that belief. As other examples, they believe that Jesus spent some time studying in Egypt and at other times, he lived with the Essenes. Finally, since the Bible states that Jesus spent time in the wilderness where the Essenes were, and since the Essenes were the second largest religious group in Judea during the life of Christ, then the New Ager is mystified as to why the Essenes are never mentioned in the Bible as being a part of the times of Jesus.

In respect to THE TEACHINGS OF CHRIST, the New Ager would accept all that was presented about the SERMONS, PARABLES, EXAMPLES and SUMMARY of the teachings of Jesus Christ. In fact, the New Ager would present the Eastern nature of the Parables as evidence about where Jesus spent the years of his life which are not recorded in the scriptures. But further, the New Ager would state that there are acceptable and meaningful teachings of Jesus which have been omitted from the accepted canon of scripture. Some of these teachings are presented in the Apocrypha, but are beyond the scope of this particular presentation.

In respect to THE CONFLICTS OF CHRIST, this section could have been written by a typical New Ager, as could THE EFFECTS OF THE CRUCIFIXION AND RESURRECTION OF JESUS CHRIST. However, the New Ager would submit that Jesus is not the only one who has ascended, even though because of his followers, the ascension of Jesus Christ has arguably had a greater effect on the people of Earth than any other recent ascension. This point is discussed further in Chapter 5.

SUMMARY

In respect to beliefs in or about Jesus Christ, there are many similarities between the typical Christian and the typical New Ager; but there also are some differences. Although many of these differences are minor and might be even less than the differences between sects within the Christian Church, others are major. These major differences are uniform and consistent, even when comparing a non-homogeneous Christian religion with an equally non-homogeneous New Age religion. These major differences are discussed further in Chapters 5, 6 and 7.

''Oh Sacrament of summer days,
Oh Last Communion in the Haze--
Permit a child to join.

Thy sacred emblems to partake--
Thy consecrated bread to take
And thine immortal wine!''

Emily Dickinson *No. 130 [Ca. 1859] st. 5,6*

''History is in a manner a sacred thing, so far as it contains
truth; for where truth is, the supreme Father of it may also be
said to be, at least, in as much as it concerns the truth''

Cervantes *Don Quixote, pt. II, bk. III, ch. 3, p. 465*

CHAPTER 4   THE SACRAMENTS

The word "Sacrament" is a noun derived from the Latin verb "sacrare" meaning "to consecrate" or "to make sacred". The word "consecrate" comes from the Latin verb *consecrare*, coming in turn from two Latin words or syllables: *com* meaning "intensive" and the familiar *sacrare*. Thus, when a sacrament is done, it is an intensively sacred act.

Most religions have had intensively sacred acts or sacraments as a part of their religious experience. In the early Christian Church, these sacraments were derived from the seven rites of the historical Christian Church which were thought to have been instituted by or observed by Jesus as a testament to inner grace or as a channel which would mediate grace. In the liturgical churches such as the Roman Catholic Church, these sacraments consist of: baptism, confirmation, the Eucharist [or Holy Communion], matrimony, orders, penance, and unction [or extreme unction]. In the reformed churches such as the Presbyterian Church, the only sacraments are baptism and communion, although the others are considered to be rites of the church. The difference between a sacrament and a rite is that in a sacrament, Grace is received by the

95

person. Grace means the "state of being protected or sanctified [made holy] by the favor of God". As an example, the Presbyterian Church believes that it has the power to perform the holy act of marrying a man and a woman, but that by doing this holy act, the two people themselves are not necessarily made holy; whereas the Roman Catholic Church believes that they are. The difference between a rite and a sacrament is the effect on the individual. The Presbyterian Church and many other Protestant churches believe that only by baptism or by communion will the individual come within the power of holy Grace and be changed or made holy; whereas the Roman Catholic Church believes that there are seven paths by which an individual can come within holy Grace. Other Christian churches classify their sacraments as being someplace in between, with some even believing that Baptism is merely a covenant or an agreement, instead of being outward evidence of a life that has been changed.

The remainder of this Chapter will discuss the meaning of the seven sacraments to both the Christian and the New Ager. The order of presentation will be alphabetical, which is the same order in which they were presented above.

BAPTISM

As a general statement, all religions consider baptism to be a sacrament. As an example of its importance to Christians, the first item in the life of Jesus Christ which is mentioned by all four Gospels is his baptism. Although three of the Gospels mention an item describing the holiness of Jesus Christ prior to his baptism, only the sacrament of baptism is mentioned in all four Gospels as being an early act during which he became holy. Because of this, baptism can be considered to be the earliest rite or sacrament in Christianity.

But baptism as a rite is much older than Christianity. Its

origin goes back to tribal religious practices which were based on pre-tribal liturgies and which were later passed down through religious practice. In its modern usage, baptism is defined as being a religious rite in which the recipient is cleansed of sin and admitted into the inner workings of his chosen religion; but the word ''baptism'' can also mean ''the first time'' as in ''baptism by fire''. The theological connotation of baptism combines these two definitions. It means the admittance of an individual into the faith for the first time by the cleansing of all past sin. In Christianity, this is done by the use of water and the recital of a form of words. Baptism into a monotheistic religion such as Christianity is a ''rite of passage'' which, once navigated successfully, need not be repeated; for that person has now, for the first time, accepted the God with whom he has been baptized. It is not a ceremony to be confused with confirmation, or with the repeatable ceremonies of reaffirmation, or even of rededication. Baptism is a ''one-time'' experience. Because of this, baptism has a truly great religious significance, probably the greatest of any of the recognized sacraments; because during baptism, the person's life is changed forever as he is enrolled into the service of his God.

Because of such a drastic change, the symbolic meaning of baptism becomes that of death and resurrection; and the rite of baptism becomes an outward sign that the person has died, and has been reborn into the religion which has baptized him. This has been true in all religions. In Judaism, circumcision is the outward sign of the inward acceptance into the faith. It is a sign of the covenant with God. It shows the death of the person who was outside of the religion, and the resurrection or rebirth of that person into the religion. The Christian rite of baptism by the use of water and words is also symbolic of the death of the old person and his rebirth by resurrection into the faith. It is an outward sign of the inner change in the person. But baptism is more than symbology. It has religious significance which has to do with the new life which the person accepts when he has been accepted by God. Possibly the most striking example of this effect is the baptism of Jesus by John the Baptist in the river Jordan. Jesus was not a noted teacher prior to having his life changed via the baptismal ceremony; but by means of this outward sign of the inner change, Jesus presented himself as being ready to do his Father's work. All who accept Christianity by being baptized in his name, accept Christ's way as their way. This new way of living is the most vital significance of the baptismal experience to the Christian.

Prior to the time that Christianity had been declared a state religion by Constantine, it was considered to be one of the mystery religions, so named because their practices were kept mysterious or secret by the use of specific initiation ceremonial rites such as baptism. Baptism was one of the more important ceremonial rites in all of the mystery religions because, as in Christianity, baptism was the rite which was most responsible for strengthening the bonds within the religious community. Unlike monotheistic Christianity, some of the mystery religions practiced henotheism--the worship of one god without denying the existence of other gods. Because other gods did exist, then baptism with the god of one mystery cult would not necessarily mean baptism with the god of another cult. And since the ceremony of baptism would differ depending on the specific mystery religion, then the baptism itself might have to be redone, even if the same God were kept. But in Christianity and in most religions which practice baptism, once the baptism has been done, then no other baptism is needed unless the person is changing his god. This specific characteristic of baptism has been generally recognized and accepted by every modern religion which practices baptism.

In the early mystery religions, baptism had symbology similar to that found in Christianity, but some went much further in relating their baptismal practices to the symbology of death and resurrection than the Judeo-Christian religions ever did. In certain mystery religions, some candidates for baptism were buried or shut up in a sarcophagus in order to symbolize death; some were symbolically deprived of their entrails and mummified, using animal entrails as the substitute for entrails removal and using drugged sleep as the substitute for mummification; some were symbolically drowned or decapitated; some symbolically had their heart removed, passed around and eaten, using an animal heart as a substitute. All of these practices were meant to represent that the initiate had left his old life and entered into a new one by the act of baptism, by the act of renouncing the old and accepting the new life in the god of his choice. This is exactly the death of the old and resurrection into the new which is represented by the Christian rite of baptism using water and words. And just like the Christian baptism, once baptized into one of the mystery religions, the rite of baptism into that specific religion need never again be repeated.

The New Ager also believes in baptism. Some of the ceremonies within the New Age religion are almost as exotic as those of the most extreme mystery schools; while others are less elaborate than those of Christianity in that they will consist only of words and not even require the use of water. And most New Agers believe in the same God represented by the Judeo-Christian heritage, whatever His name may be. Consequently, like the Christian, the New Ager will feel the need for only one baptism; for once baptized, he will have dedicated himself to the service of the God in whose name he was baptized. And unless that dedication has been renounced by active dedication to something else or by the person feeling that he did not really mean it in the first place, then the act of baptism need never again be repeated, for although God may miss His children if they are neglectful, He would never forget them.

However, both the Christian and the New Ager may forget God or neglect His activities or make vacant His place in their lives. Therefore, they may feel the need to reestablish contact with the God to whom they have dedicated themselves by reaffirming their

faith as an outward sign of their inner commitment; or by rededi-
cating themselves to the Master whom they are dedicated to serve,
but whom they have neglected in the hassle of their day-after-day
life. But they do not need to be baptized again; for if a human
remains dedicated to that God to whom he first expressed dedication by being baptized, then he has been baptized for all the time that
he is a human, and probably for long after that. That is the difference
between baptism and rededication. Once baptized, that is not all
there is. After baptism comes living the life in the way that it has
been dedicated, and possibly rededicated, and even rerededicated.
But not rebaptized, for there is no such thing in Christianity or in
any other sacrament-oriented religion.

CONFIRMATION

Confirmation is another sacrament or rite of the Christian
church. During confirmation, a person is admitted into the full
membership of the church by reaffirming the vows made by him or
for him at his baptism. By the rite of confirmation, a person who
had been welcomed into the family of the church by infant baptism
can state for himself that the baptismal vows accepted by others for
him are accepted by that person. It may be that a person may feel
that he had not truly entered into the baptism when done the first
time, and must enter into that ceremony once again; but this is not
the rite of confirmation. Instead, this would be a "first time"
baptism and a true one this time. Once truly baptized into any faith,
the rite of baptism need not be repeated, although it may be
confirmed as an act of public testimony or otherwise reaffirmed if
the need is felt, or rededicated if the attention has slipped.

Within the Christian Church, confirmation can range from
an extremely elaborate ceremony to the mere statement of a few
words of belief; and the same is true for the New Age religion.
Within some Christian churches, it is believed that the person is

made holy by entering into the Confirmation procedure; but within others, whereas Confirmation is a holy act, it is believed that doing it does not make the person holy. The some range of beliefs can be found within the New Age religion. Within most Christian churches, confirmation can be repeated as often as needed; and the same is true within the New Age.

COMMUNION

The sacrament of the Communion or Holy Communion is also known as the Eucharist. It is the Christian sacrament which commemorates the Last Supper which Jesus Christ had with his disciples. At the Last Supper, it is recorded that "Now as they were eating, Jesus took bread, and blessed, and broke it, and gave it to the disciples and said, 'Take, eat; this is my body.' And he took a cup, and when he had given thanks he gave it to them, saying, 'Drink of it, all of you; for this is my blood of the covenant, which is poured out for many for the forgiveness of sins. I tell you I shall not drink again of this fruit of the vine until that day when I drink it new with you in my Father's kingdom' " [Matthew 26: 26-30]. The sacrament of Communion, a rite which is considered a sacrament in most Christian churches, is a reenactment of that particular occurrence.

Within Christianity, there is an extreme range of beliefs concerning this sacrament. At one extreme, some of these beliefs present the certainty that in the blessing of the bread, that element is converted into the actual body of the Christ; and in the giving of thanks for the wine, that element is converted into the actual blood of the Christ. Each of these is then taken into the actual body of the Communicant; and since these elements are actually converted, then all must be consumed by a believer, and not merely thrown away in the garbage. At the other extreme, there is the belief that the bread remains bread and the wine remains wine or is actually grape juice, each of which represents merely a remembrance of

101

Christ's presence at the Last Supper. And between these extremes, all sorts of middle grounds exist.

But again, most Christian churches consider this rite to be a sacrament, meaning that those who partake are sanctified or made holy by the process. This particular Act of Faith has always been one of the most difficult of all Christian concepts for the non-Christian to accept. Some have even believed it to be witchcraft or to be cannibalistic in nature.

Since this rite or sacrament is unique to a specific event which happened in the Christian heritage and in no other, then there is no corresponding ceremony within the New Age religion, except by those who are practicing Christians while also holding some New Age beliefs.

MATRIMONY

"Matrimony" refers to the state of being married with emphasis on its religious nature; whereas "wedlock" refers to the same state, but with emphasis on its legal nature. In each reference, contemporary standards generally assume the married state to be that of one man with one woman; whereas standards not generally accepted could relate to a married state between more than one of each sex with one of the other sex, or the married state between members of the same sex, or communal living of all people "married" to all others whatever the number or sexual mixture.

At the present time, Christian churches generally recognize only the one man-one woman kind of marriage; although a tremendous pressure is being exerted to recognize "same sex marriages". At the present time, only the one man-one woman kind of marriage has legal recognition within the state; but again pressure is being applied to recognize "same sex marriages". At the present time, only religions recognized by the state can perform legally recognized marriages; but again, pressure is being applied to broaden the religious spectrum which would be accepted. As other examples, marriage performed by a legal representative such as a Justice of the Peace or the Captain of an ocean-going ship is accepted by almost all representatives of the state as being a legal union: whereas such a marriage is accepted by some Christian churches and not accepted by others. And finally, some Christian churches believe that by participating in the marriage ceremony, the people being married are made holy; whereas others do not express this belief. Possibly no human endeavor is so confusing as the human definition of ''what God has joined together''.

No New Age religion is recognized as a religion by the state. Consequently, no marriage rites can be performed which are legally recognized. In some New Age religions, marriage vows are exchanged which are later made legally recognized by a ceremony conducted in the presence of a legal representative; or which are made legally recognized as a ''common law'' marriage as accepted by some states. However, the phrase ''what God has joined together'' has a meaning in the New Age religion which goes much deeper than any similar expression used in any Christian church; for many New Agers believe in being joined together throughout eternity, which is a much deeper commitment than the '' 'til death do us part'' phrase used by most Christian churches.

ORDERS

Orders or Holy Orders is considered to be a sacrament in the Catholic and Orthodox churches, but rarely in any other Christian church. Orders are considered to have gained their authority from the concept of apostolic succession, an idea originally developed in the second century to verify Christian teaching as superior to that of the Gnostics, a sect who believed that salvation comes from esoteric knowledge rather than from faith. Apostolic succession granted the legitimacy of office holders by the laying on of hands through a chain that symbolically reached back to the Apostles. Such Orders then allowed a person to exercise the power of the office into which he had been ordained. In the Roman Catholic Church, there are four minor orders [porter, reader, exorcist and acolyte] and four major orders [subdeacon, deacon, priest, and bishop]; but only the last three are considered to be sacramental, *i.e.* granting holiness to the individual receiving the Order.

Although Protestant churches do not normally have Orders as a sacrament, they often will practice the rite of ordaining [*i.e.* installing] ministers or church officers such as deacons, elders or the like. In this rite, the person being ordained is recognized as having the authority to undertake certain functions, but is not considered to be any more holy than he was prior to ordination. As some examples of the authority which ordination will confer, in general only ordained ministers will have the authority to perform marriages, to serve Communion or the like; and only ordained Deacons or Elders will have the authority to vote on certain church matters. But again, unlike Roman Catholicism, Protestants who have been ordained are considered to be no more holy because of the ordination than they were before they were ordained.

To the New Ager, ordination is a sacrament second in importance only to baptism. In general, the ordination will be to that of a priest or a priestess in an Order, such as the Order of Michael, the Order of Melchizedek or the like. In general there will be 12 levels of ordination in any Order, and 12 steps of achievement within each level. Each of these 144 steps will confer not only additional authority on the initiate who has been ordained, but also will confer additional difficulty in achieving the tasks which are assigned. In some New Age cults, the tasks are assigned by an earthly leader; but in the less well known and possibly more enlightened New Age sects, the tasks come solely from the soul consciousness of the individual as it works directly with his God.

Despite its importance as a sacrament to many New Agers, most individuals who have New Age religious beliefs do not belong to any particular Order, and thus do not participate in any Ordination ceremonies.

PENANCE

Penance was originally required because of the belief that a serious sinner would not be welcome to receive the body and the blood of the Christ during Communion. Consequently, the sacrament of Penance was established to allow the sinner to publicly repent of his sins by undergoing a period of public penance such as fasting, the wearing of sackcloth or the like. Capital sins such as murder, adultery and the like often were not forgiven by penance, meaning that although God may be able to forgive, the local church was not; and therefore the individual had permanently lost his standing in the church. By the Middle Ages, public penance was replaced by confession to the Priest and by receiving the Priest's absolution. In addition, the possibility of replacing Penance by an Indulgence was established. An Indulgence is a declaration by the church that certain officially listed prayers and /or good works can substitute for Penance. Abuse of the Indulgence system was one of the major causes of the Reformation and the formation of Protestant churches.

Protestant churches tend to speak of repentance rather than Penance. By this they mean a sincere remorse for sinful deeds and the sincere desire to obey the command of Jesus Christ when he said, "Neither do I condemn you; go, and do not sin again." [John 8:11]. However some Protestant sects such as the Anabaptists and the Quakers continue to accept public Penance as a rite approaching a sacrament.

Although some of the extreme "mind-control" type of cults which are often classified as a part of the New Age movement

105

are very active in the use of public penance, in general, the more enlightened sects have no such rite. Penance is simply not needed for two reasons: [1] to impart penance would require making a judgment, and few New Agers believe that they have the right to judge one another; and [2] a large number of New Agers, possibly the majority, do not believe in sin.

EXTREME UNCTION

Unction, or Extreme Unction, or the Anointing of the Sick is justified by the Bible as in James 5:14-5 which says, "Is any among you sick? Let him call for the elders of the church, and let them pray over him, anointing him with oil in the name of the Lord; and the prayer of faith will save the sick man, and the Lord will raise him up; and if he has committed sins, he will be forgiven." It became a very important sacrament for the early church, for it was to be given only to those who were seriously ill, with "serious" meaning "close to death". It was an important sacrament because there was a belief that any residual sins would sap the spiritual resources needed to successfully resist the illness, and thus the anointing and the forgiveness of sins would either cure the patient, or prepare him for his death, either of which was desirable. It has rarely if ever been considered to be a sacrament in the Protestant churches.

The New Ager would never consider the Anointing of the Sick to be a sacrament for two reasons: [1] his belief about sin, and [2] his belief about death. These subjects will be discussed in greater detail in Chapters 5-7.

SUMMARY

Although there are differences between Christianity and the New Age in relation to those acts which are considered to be sacred acts or sacraments, the difference within Christianity is greater than the difference between the Protestants and the New Agers. Although some adherents will disagree, in general both Protestants and New Agers believe that there are two sacred acts. In the case of Protestantism, these two sacraments are Baptism and Communion; whereas in New Age they are Baptism and Ordination. In general, each sacrament is a devotion to the same God.

"...on the principle of the iceberg. There is seven-eighths of it under water for every part that shows. Anything you know you can eliminate and it only strengthens your iceberg. It is the part that doesn't show...."

Ernest Hemingway *Interview, Paris Review [Spring, 1958]*

"...but go to my brethren and say to them, I am ascending to my Father and your Father, to my God and your God."
The Bible, <u>The Gospel According to John</u>, 20:17

"And now I will ascend to God, as you and all the world will rise to God."
The Aquarian Gospel of Jesus the Christ, Chapter 180:16

"And Jesus will shine more radiantly than at the hour when he ascended to the heavens, so that the Light will melt into a rainbow as Brother and Sister step forth 'in a flash of Light' to be with the Lords already in the Light.
The Keys of Enoch, Key 3-1-6:16

CHAPTER 5   NEW AGE BELIEFS

The New Age movement is relatively new with no uniformly established doctrines and no universally accepted writings. In this instance, it is somewhat like the Christian movement of about 50 AD or so. Since it is still a collection of individual people rather than of doctrines to which all individual people must adhere, the movement is not uniform in its beliefs; and any attempt to define the basic beliefs upon which the movement is based will present conclusions which are tenuous at best, and upon which not all will agree. Nevertheless, an attempt should be made, for any movement which does not try to delineate its initial beliefs has no reason to depict itself as a movement.

This Chapter will attempt to define the basic beliefs of the New Age movement by first addressing what the movement does not accept about itself, followed by what it does. There is no question that those reading this Chapter will express a lot of doubt or disbelief, just as a citizen of Rome, the then greatest nation in the world, would have expressed a lot of doubt or disbelief if he were to have read the Apostles' Creed during the summer of 51 AD; but the New Age faithful have a belief about the statements in this Chapter which is just as sincere as the beliefs expressed by Paul,

Peter and the others some two thousand years ago.

There is one more point to be made before proceeding into this Chapter, and that is the Fact that Beliefs are not Facts [see Chapter 1]. This Chapter presents Beliefs; and although some might like these beliefs to be converted into facts by the use of our limited five physical senses, remember the words of Jesus Christ who said, "Have you believed because you have seen me? Blessed are those who have not seen and yet believe." [John 20: 29] Although this quotation refers to a particular incident in the ministry of Jesus and in the life of Thomas, it is a good lesson to accept; because it states that whereas facts can often be verified by having been seen, heard, smelled, tasted or touched, many times beliefs can not. This Chapter is on the beliefs of the New Ager.

MISCONCEPTIONS

There are three major conclusions which investigators of the New Age movement seem to have developed after taking a somewhat hurried or cursory look. Most New Agers do not accept these conclusions. These conclusions are:

1. That the movement is primarily concerned with Mind Control;
2. That the movement exists solely in esoteric cults which worship Satan; and
3. That the movement is Eastern in its thinking and thus is non-Christian.

MIND CONTROL In a book originally published in 1977 and republished in 1989, the following paragraph appears:

"Sebottendorff's Fuhrerprinzip is basic to esoteric cults. The disciple must blindly obey his master, who not only has secret knowledge, hidden from the initiate, but who must create favorable conditions in which his pupil can undergo a drastic change. This allows for actions which violate individual conscience.''[12]

Later, in the same book, the following paragraph appears:
''If we are to ask now, more than a generation later, how normal people could have committed the Nazi atrocities, we need only look at the normal people in American cults today. This may seem like a harsh comparison; the parallels are certainly not universally applicable. Still, it would not be unfair to say that the same sort of normal people who obeyed the crazy commands of the Nazi hierarchy are today obeying the crazy commands of some contemporary cult leaders. To be sure, those commands, apart from certain Satanic cults, do not call for ritual murder. Not yet, at any rate. But none of us should feel too comfortable with so many of our compatriots so willing to suspend independent judgment, and so ill equipped to exercise that judgment.''[13]

Later, in the same book, the following paragraph appears:
''I have been present at meetings where proselytes, presumably sane and rational, accepted without question irrational doctrines presented portentously, believing that they were receiving revealed truth.''[14]

The author then goes on to mention Charles Manson with his ''cult'', the Reverend Sun Myung Moon with the ''Moonies'', L. Ron Hubbard with ''Scientology'', Werner Hans Erhard with ''EST'', and the like as being representative leaders of the New Age movement who foster Mind Control as a part of their leadership practice.

Several mature New Agers were asked whether or not their beliefs had been expressed in these paragraphs. This was not done in an attempt to discredit in any way the opinions of others; but merely to get a feel about the New Age belief system. Without exception, the response was that their belief system differed from this presentation. To a great extent, the mature New Ager believes in the individual and his soul to such a great extent, that to suspend independent judgment and to let his mind be controlled by another would be completely out of the question. All New Age belief is not represented by Manson, Moon and Hubbard any more than all Christianity is represented by Torquemada who ran the Spanish Inquisition in the 16th Century, or by Samuel Sewall who was one of the judges at the Salem Witch Trials in the late 17th century, or by the mind control represented by the "eternal damnation" sermons of many Christian preachers. Every religion has its bad moments, for there have been atrocities committed in the name of every religion on the face of this earth. As a few examples, in the first Century after the coming of the "true Christian God", fifty million Mayan people, fully 90% of the population died. To the Mayan, the coming of the "true God" brought extortion, killing and misery.[15] And the situation in India once got so far out of control during the time that one religion was trying to force its "true religion" on another, that even the peacemaker Mahatma Ghandi said, "Religion itself is outraged when outrage is committed in its name"; and in that same vein, he said, "All religions are true." And finally, there is no doubt that the massacre at the Peoples Temple in Jonestown, Guyana was caused by some who claimed to be of the New Age.

But it is not the intent of this book to "throw stones" or to argue opinions. Instead, the intent is to try to inform or to generate some understanding. The majority of the New Age belief system does not include mind control of any sort. Instead, the study of the New Age belief system tends to free the mind. In addition, New Agers feel that their efforts are for the betterment of all mankind. If this were not true, it would indeed be a frightening thought, for the power of a freed mind can indeed be an awesome thing.

SATANISM   In the book previously mentioned, the following paragraphs appear:

"Membership in occult groups in America today has reached epidemic proportions. Some people take this as an omen that Satan is hard at work; others that God is. The groups take many different forms: Satanism, witchcraft, pseudoscience, mind-control, mysticism, Christian, pagan. Most are not as innocent as they seem, as we are beginning to find out.

The one that has been most often compared with the Nazis is, of course, the Charles Manson cult, with its murderous violence and sadomasochistic sex. All the Satanic groups express a great admiration for Hitler. Anton LaVey, the leader of the Church of Satan, probably has the largest collection of Nazi memorabilia in America. LaVey dedicated his book The Satanic Bible to a number of people, including the Nazi geopolitician 'Karl Haushofer, a teacher without a classroom'"[16]

Another recent book [1991] is The Hiding Places of God, subtitled "A Personal Journey into the World of Religious Visions, Holy Objects and Miracles". In this excellent work by an investigative reporter, 288 pages are used to investigate thoroughly almost every Roman Catholic vision or mystical experience; whereas six pages are contained in a chapter entitled "Satanism and the New Age" in which the New Age is addressed only in superficial generalities, and almost always is associated with the specifics of Satanism.[17]

Satanism is not a product of New Age beliefs, for the worship of Satan by those who would choose to do so has been around for a lot longer than the New Age. And the New Age beliefs are not a product of Satanism, as those who continue to read this Chapter will possibly discern. It is probable that the emphasis on the unsavory practices of those who become Ego-centered rather than God-centered is merely an echo of conventional reporting. People seem to desire to read negative reports rather than positive ones. As a few examples, what stories tend to make headlines and to sell papers--the 99% of the Christian ministers who do their job for God each day, or the Bakers and the Swaggarts; the 95% [or more] of the people who hug their kids at night, or the ones who beat them; the 93% of the people who have jobs, or the headlines that shout that ''Unemployment reaches 7.1%''??? This is not to say that a society should not try to unmask the culprits, to jail the abusers, and to generate jobs for those who need them; but to categorize all of Christianity, or of parenthood, or of employers by the headline-making actions of the minority is more sensationalism than responsibility. The responsible New Ager is well aware of the misuse which could be done with the power of his beliefs. And the responsible New Ager is also well aware that most of the examples of mind control or Satanic practices occur when the individual lets Ego replace Spirit as his guide. There will be more on this subject later in this Chapter and in Chapters 6 and 7.

EASTERN THOUGHTS   Two books [18,19] have been published which present a fundamentalist Christian viewpoint about the New Age cults or religions. The first was published in 1980 and the second in 1990. Each book evaluates all the identified New Age sects and comments on their acceptability to Christians. One of the recurring themes regarding the unacceptability of most of the sects has to do with their Eastern religious practices such as meditation, Pantheism, chanting and the like. This subject will be discussed more thoroughly in Chapter 7; but for the present, it should be noted that the New Ager feels that in its original practice before it was organized and Westernized by Rome, Christianity was very much an Eastern religion. To substantiate this belief, one does not need to resort to the Apocrypha, or to the Hindu texts, or to the readings of Edgar Cayce all of which describe the time that Jesus spent in India and Persia; instead one needs merely read the Bible, and particularly the esoteric teachings of the Parables which constitute most of Jesus' recorded teachings. The Parables are very Eastern in nature [see Chapter 3] and very esoteric [meaning to be understood only by a few or to be understood on many different levels] in their approach [see Mark 4:12]. Consequently, it is not a misconception that the New Age religion has an Eastern background; it is a misconception that Christianity does not.

BELIEFS

The New Age group of individuals is a very diverse group. As such, it will be difficult to cover all the possible beliefs without omitting some possibilities. In addition, it will be difficult to cover the chosen ones in a way that could satisfy all the New Agers in all of their various stages of development. Consequently, this Chapter should be considered to be only an overview which will try to paint a general picture of the beliefs of the New Ager. It will do so by addressing five important beliefs: [1] Soul, [2] Time, [3] Dimensions, [4] Ascensions, and [5] Unconditional Love. One other concept or belief is so important and fundamental that it will be addressed separately in Chapter 6. It is the Experiences of the Presence of God.

SOUL The New Ager believes that he, and all other entities made in the image of the Creator God [Genesis 1:27], have an eternal Soul which is a part of them, and an eternal Spirit which is a part of the God which created them. In addition, when each individual entity incarnates, it exists and can function in four bodies: the physical, the mental, the emotional and the spiritual. These four bodies are bound together by the Soul. The goal of the Soul is to balance these four bodies in such a way that the entity is not ruled by one alone, but by a perfect harmony or balance between the four. The Soul does this by gaining and resolving experiences, both when incarnate and when not. The goal of the Spirit is to bring the Soul into perfect harmony or balance with the Creator. The Spirit does this by guiding the Soul into the free will choices which are on the path to oneness with the Creator.

Some New Agers believe that all Souls have existed since the Beginning, just as the Soul of Jesus had. Others believe that new Souls have been and will be created as God expands and grows. Either belief is useful for what has to be done in the now; for in either case, there are experiences to be gained and resolved in order to have the Soul continue along the pathway to oneness. It is of interest to note that this same debate [i.e. do souls pre-exist] raged throughout Christianity during its first 400 years of existence as represented by the conflict between the teachings of Origen and the actions of Justinian among others [see Chapter 7].

Most New Agers believe that the Soul, when originally created, was created without sex, just as God is without sex even though New Agers tend to refer to God as He/She or as Father/Mother and the Jesuit priest Andrew Greeley always calls God ''She'' in his novels. The New Ager believes that in order to gain the required experiences, the Soul incarnates into both the male and female forms [see Genesis 1:27 for a biblical parallelism] and at various times will possess either predominately male or predominately female qualities. Some New Agers believe that this division was a semi-permanent thing and that one of the goals for an individualized entity is to find his/her ''twin flame'' which is the other half of his/her Soul. In this manner, the Soul can then be made whole for subsequent Spirit-directed oneness with the Creator. In the meantime, the Soul and the Spirit work with the separated soul mates as they gain and resolve experiences. Other New Agers believe that the soul does not divide but instead resides within the one entity and that the balance [or adrogyny] comes not from finding a ''twin flame'' from outside of self, but from balancing the male/female qualities within self in order to be made whole for subsequent Spirit-directed oneness with God. In either case, there is the desire to come into the oneness of God by creating a balance

116

between the male/female qualities and thus become as God, *i.e.* without one sex being in an imbalance with the other. The Soul works with Spirit to generate the experiences required to have this happen.

As a more complete explanation of the New Ager's concept of the Soul, it should be understood that the Soul is the first evolving structure of life. It evolves from a Group to become an individualized Soul. It then gains further evolution by experiences gained through incarnation and reincarnation. During these incarnations, the entity or personality generates more intelligence which the soul puts together as it evolves. Many established religions have, in many ways, led us to believe that the Soul is perfect and is with God in heaven. The New Ager does not accept this; for since the Soul needs experiences to gain evolution toward oneness, then it cannot be perfect as yet. And in addition, the New Ager feels that short of the final death, there is no such thing as perfection anyway; for if God in Heaven were perfect, He would stop evolving and would crystallize or have final death. So the New Ager believes that the more he integrates the parts that his Soul puts together as unresolved experiences, the more that he is being supportive as an energy field for the expansion of the Soul. In return, the entity or personality shares then the greater part of the Soul's intelligence and uses it in the way that it continues to process and integrate experiences. The more experiences the Soul has, the more it can integrate unresolved experiences into the evolution toward oneness.

It is obvious that the New Ager feels that the Soul plays an extremely important role in his eternal life; for as it accepts Spirit's guidance for the eternal journey of the entity, the Soul helps to pose a powerful deterrent to participation in activities such as mind control or the worship of Satan. For such participation, Ego may have replaced Spirit in the guidance process. When that happens, Soul and Spirit work to bring the entity out of an Ego-centered direction, and back to guidance by Spirit.

TIME Obviously, for the Soul to do all of these things, it takes more time than merely a single lifetime. Consequently, over an eternity, the Soul will come into an incarnation [*i.e.* it will enter into a physical body], will gain the experiences programmed for it by its Soul during that incarnation, will leave the body behind in order to gain understanding about what has been experienced and what still remains unresolved, and will then return to another physical body [*i.e.* it will reincarnate] in order to gain more experience and to resolve those things which have been left unresolved. After a finite time on planet Earth and through an eternity on other, higher frequency planes, the Soul will evolve through progress toward oneness with the Creator, but will never get there. That is one definition of an eternity, for although an entity might be where God was, it can never be where God is, since by the evolution gained by the entity, God has also grown and evolved. For God cannot remain static. If He did, then He would crystallize and be alive no more. Then we would truly be at the ''God is dead'' stage-- a stage which has never existed in the past, and hopefully will never exist in the future.

Because of this belief in Time, the New Ager will submit that entities have been around for a much longer period than most historians will admit. In recent times, these entities have existed as people in something such as their present form; but the New Ager submits that even this form has existed for a much longer period than most historians will admit. In a sermon in a Christian church, a highly respected minister once referred to the time of David as having been ''ancient days''. It is believed [though not proved] that David lived in about 1,000 BC or so. If so, then the ''ancient days'' mentioned by the minister occurred about 3,000 years ago. It is generally believed [though not proved] that the earth has existed in essentially its present spot in relation to the Universe for about 4 billion years. This means that the earth had been in existence for

118

99.999925% of its present existence before those ''ancient days'' occurred! Because of this extensive existence, isn't it possible that something happened before those ''ancient days''--something which has been forgotten by the human memory? And don't submit that history would have recorded it; for today, we still argue about what really happened during the American Civil War, or in the administration of Warren G. Harding, or in Dallas on November 22, 1963; and certainly none of these can be described as being ''ancient days''. History, even recent history, is simply not as specific as we would like to think.

Let us let our mind wander for a moment about the possible effect of catastrophes. What if a collision between Earth and a gigantic meteorite were to occur today, and this collision were so great that it would erase all forms of life, incinerate all combustible material such as wood, paper, computer cables and the like, and melt all metallic substances? What if there were nothing left on Earth except stone? And what if, after a relatively short period of say 10,000 years, some form of life began to appear which evolved for enough time that it again became civilized? In its records or in the records of the parts of dry earth which were available to that new civilization, would they find any record of us? Or do the same thing with an Ice Age so intense that it caused the Earth to rotate on its axis such that Miami would become the North Pole and would be buried under many miles of ice. Would that new civilization find what had once been known as Miami Beach? Or do the same thing with a volcanic eruption in the middle of the Atlantic Ocean such that a major new continent rose, thus inundating all of the United States east of the Rockies. Would a civilization of 10,000 years in the future remember anything about the Empire State building? And what is an Empire State anyway?

In the incredibly long [in human historical terms] age of the Earth, each of these catastrophes could have happened. Each is a possibility. Since each would have left us with little or no record of

119

what had transpired before, and since many New Agers seem to have a nagging memory about pre-historical events from some sort of primal consciousness, then the typical New Ager believes in "ancient days" from much further back than that mentioned by the minister. For example, the New Ager believes that there was a populated land of Lemuria some 80,000 years ago, and a dry land of Atlantis some 10-16,000 years ago. In addition, he believes that even these may be recent occurrences based on many things such as the imprint of a sewn moccasin which became fossilized under the fossil of a small animal which hasn't existed on Earth for over 200 million years! Incidentally, although 200 million years may seem like a long time, at that point in geological time, the Earth had already been around for 95% of its present age!

For many reasons, the New Ager has quite an expanded idea of Time in relation to human consciousness.

DIMENSIONS If any one subject were to be considered unique to the New Ager and thus able to classify him as being different than other people whether in respect to religion or to humanity, it would be the subject of dimensions. It is the one belief which pulls together the possibility of all the others.

To understand the concept of dimensions which is unique to the New Ager, there has to be some understanding of light. Like electricity [see Chapter 2], we don't know very much about light. In the latter part of the 19th century, a furious debate was being carried on by physicists. Some thought that light was a wave; whereas others thought it was a photon. One of the most famous unsuccessful experiments of all time was conducted by Michelson and Morly in Cleveland in 1887. It was designed to prove once and for all whether light was a wave or a photon. The experiment proved that it was neither--or both. Even today we don't know much more; for we only know that under certain conditions, light responds as if it were a wave, and under other conditions, as if it were photonic. Even now, our best simple description of light is that it is energy--pure energy--which can be used in many diverse ways. Of course, in this sense, light is not only the light which we can see, but includes all of the electromagnetic spectrum.

In general, light is dimensionless and has no mass. Of course, the wavelengths of light do have very specific wavelengths which range all the way from the long wavelengths of the reds to the short wavelengths of the violets within the visible spectrum; and which extend into the longer infrareds or the shorter ultraviolets as the visible spectrum is left. But in the sense that it is pure energy, it is dimensionless and without mass. Light has a place in the Bible. In the very first verses of Genesis, the Bible says that first there was God, who then created light, and who then created things. This could be paraphrased to say that first there was God who made energy and then used this energy to make things which have mass. This interpretation fits very well into the ''Big Bang'' theory of modern physics which, when applied to the creation of physical things, states that first, there was just energy; and then the energy got together in such a way that every physical thing that has ever been created was created from that energy within a very short time period--within the microscopic part of a second. From that time on, from about 18 billion years ago or so, there have been no new physical things created, just rearrangements of the physical things that have existed since the incident of the ''Big Bang''. The physical possibility of such an occurrence was first predicted by Einstein. In one application of his Theory of Relativity, it was predicted that mass could be converted into energy, and vice versa. Turning mass into energy creates an atomic bomb; whereas turning energy into mass creates the physical universe.

What is energy? In a classical sense, energy is defined as the equivalent of or the capacity for doing work. It can be associated with a material body such as a coiled and set spring; or it can be independent of matter such as light in a vacuum. Energy leads to power which is defined as the rate of doing work and therefore the rate of energy flow. Since one definition of God is that He is omnipotent [see Chapter 2] which means "having all power", this series of definitions leads to a definition of God which says that He has control of all of the rates of energy flow. And this, when combined with dimensions, is a definition of God which fits with the New Ager very well. The New Ager sees energy flow as being the highest when the entity is in the spiritual form and the lowest when the entity is in the physical form. He sees the spiritual form as being so multi-dimensional that it is dimensionless in terms of our dimensional physical limitations. He sees God as a spirit, for as Jesus said, "God is spirit, and those who worship him must worship in spirit and truth." [John 4:24]; and as a spirit, He must be of the highest energy flow, which is energy itself--multi-dimensional energy from which all things can be made, and out of which all things may be said to exist. And yet, to those of similar multi-dimensional vibrations, the spirit would exist as an entity--as a God who was a person.

This latter point is an important one, for the New Ager's belief in dimensions goes further than merely his understanding of the form of God. It goes to an understanding of all unseen things, or of all things which occupy a different dimensional warp than our present restrictive three-dimensional physical plane. The New Ager understands that the present physical form into which his soul has incarnated is a three dimensional one having length, width, and breadth. Thus, this physical form can be seen by the existing physical senses. A one-dimensional object would have only one dimension and thus could not be seen by our physical senses, only by our mind or our mental senses. For although the geometrical representation of a one-dimensional object is a point, it is not a point like the period on a piece of paper. That point has three dimensions. However the one-dimensional object can be visualized in our mind, and in doing so, we can do something with it. In a similar sense, a two-dimensional object also could not be seen by our physical senses because although it would have length and width, it would have no height and thus would not exist to our physical senses, but only in our mind. For although the geometrical representation of a two-dimensional object is a line, it is not a line such as the underlining of a word. That line has three dimensions. However, again a two-dimensional object could be visualized in our mind, and once visualized, we could describe it or do something else with it. Only when an object gets into the third dimension is it capable of being discerned by our limited physical senses. The geometrical representation of a three dimensional object is a plane, and it can be readily be seen by the use of our physical senses. Of course, we can also visualize three dimensional objects in our mind. We can therefore describe three-dimensional objects either from our physical or from our mental capabilities. In some circles, the fourth dimension is defined as being time, for if you wish to locate a moving object, you need more than just the three dimensions of location. You also need to know when it will be there in order to see it. There is no use knowing that an airplane will be 25,000 feet over a certain latitude and longitude unless you also know when it will be there. Otherwise, if you know only the three dimensions and not the fourth, the airplane would be invisible to you unless you were lucky enough to guess the fourth dimension and be looking not only at the correct three dimensional coordinates, but also doing it at the right fourth dimension--at the right time. In a similar manner, the normally three-dimensional blades of a spinning fan will disappear because the physical eye can not time them properly. Of course, if you know what kind of an airplane it is, or can remember how the stationary blades looked, then you could mentally visualize these four-dimensional objects at any time.

It would seem fairly simple for a human caught in this three dimensional world to see how anything in a one- or two-dimensional world would be invisible to his physical senses, but might be captured by his mental senses. It also seems fairly simple for such a human to see how he could see things in a three- or four-dimensional world, but only if he knew what those three- or four-dimensions were so that he could place himself to be at the right spot at the right time. At the present time, physics has not defined the fifth or higher dimensions, but it should be fairly simple for a human caught in this three dimensional world to accept that an object operating in the fifth [or higher] dimension would not be discernible as a physical object to his physical senses. It might be available as a mental object to his mental senses, or it might even conceivably be available as an emotional object to his emotional senses, or as a spiritual object to his spiritual senses; but it would never be physically seen, heard, tasted, smelled or felt.

During prayer or meditation, have you ever heard God speak to you? Many Christians and New Agers have. And yet, it was not a physical voice, nor was it imagination. But it was something which touched the Soul with a definite message. Or have you ever felt love? With what physical sense did you feel love? Or was it of such a nature that its dimensions were beyond that of the three-dimensional physical world? And yet, wasn't it real?

The New Ager believes that God is a higher dimension being than the three or possibly four dimensions which fit into our three dimensional world. In fact, the New Ager believes that God is of such a high frequency of energy, that He is beyond dimensions, meaning that He is capable of assuming any dimension He wishes including the fourth dimension of time. This allows Him to fit the second and third definitions of God-- those of being ''all knowing'' and ''in all places'' [see Chapter 2]. In addition, the New Ager believes that there are other beings who are in dimensions both higher and lower than the three dimensions which we have as our low-frequency physical state. Some of those beings are locked into their dimensions just as our present physical forms are locked into our three dimensions; whereas others are able to go into of out of those dimensions at will because they are multidimensional. As one minor example of the usefulness of multidimensionality, this would be the only way that meaningful extraterrestrial travel could be possible--by going into a frequency dimension which is higher than the slowly vibrating three dimensional physical world into which all of our matter belongs. Staying three-dimensional is just too slow for meaningful space travel!

If a three-dimensional being can mentally or emotionally visualize dimensions to which his physical presence can not take him, then many puzzling things become explainable. Why, for example, are extraterrestrial sightings sometimes physical and sometimes not? Do they merely slip into dimensions unavailable to our physical senses? Or how could Jesus ascend when his followers seemingly could not? Did he merely follow his available capabilities by going multi-dimensional? And why can some people seemingly see Mother Mary, while others can not? Is she merely bringing parts of them up into a dimension unavailable to all? And did the entities who lived in Lemuria or Atlantis necessarily have to have the same limited three-dimensional physical form we presently have; or could they have had a form which was more compatible with the Earth of that time--possibly a form which was more etheric in its dimensions as the Earth possibly was? And when the paranormal happens and has been accepted not to be involved in some sort of chicanery, has the experience been dimensionally related? And finally, wasn't Billy Graham talking about dimensionality when he said, ''Angels speak. They appear and reappear. They feel apt sense of emotion. While angels may become visible by choice, our eyes are not constructed to see them ordinarily any more than we can see the dimensions of a nuclear field, the structure of atoms, or the electricity that flows through copper wiring. Our ability to sense reality is limited...''[20]

The New Ager not only believes in the probability of dimensionality which can apply to all of this, he also believes that at long last, progress is being made toward raising the frequencies of the Earth-bound entities, and in fact of the entire planet, to a point at which the slow and limiting three-dimensional warp will be removed to be replaced by higher vibrations which are more compatible with the more light-filled entities of the universe. This possibility is an Article of Faith as described in Chapter 6.

ASCENSIONS As the Soul passes through eternity, accepting experiences through multiple incarnations, assimilating, resolving and integrating those experiences with Spirit's guidance, and raising its vibrations into dimensions not available to the three dimensional physical form, at some point it will Ascend into those new dimensions.

The New Agers believe in ascension. They believe that Enoch ascended, for it is recorded that, "Enoch walked with God; and he was not, for God took him" [Genesis 5: 24]. They believe that Melchizedek ascended, for it is recorded that, "He is without father or mother or genealogy, and he has neither beginning of days nor end of life, but resembling the Son of God, he continues a priest forever" [Hebrews 7: 3]. They believe that the poor man, Lazarus ascended, for it is recorded that, "The poor man died and was carried by the angels to Abraham's bosom" [Luke 16: 22]. They believe that Elijah ascended, for it is recorded that "...Elijah went up by a whirlwind into heaven" [2 Kings 2:11]. They believe that Jesus ascended, for it is recorded that, "While he blessed them, he parted from them, and was carried up into heaven" [Luke 24: 51]. They believe that the angels ascend, for as Billy Graham said, "Intrinsically, angels do not possess physical bodies, although they may take on physical bodies when God appoints them to special tasks."[21] They believe that in the Apocrypha, there are many instances of ascension, just as there are in modern non-biblical writings.

Furthermore, the New Ager believes that although there

126

are many examples of ascension recorded in Judeo-Christian writings, ascension is a natural progression of any enlightened Soul and not a phenomena reserved for the privileged few. The New Ager believes that Buddha served humanity by bringing his enlightenment to those who needed it at that time, and who still need it because of where their Soul is. And therefore the New Ager believes that Buddha has ascended, as has Krishna, Mohammad and many others. The New Ager does not believe that ascension creates a God, any more than Lazarus became a God; but he does believe that ascension gives the Creator additional multidimensional helpers to carry out His work, whatever that work may be. And these helpers can do tasks or perform duties by using talents not available to those who are caught in the three-dimensional warp of this planet. The criticism by some that the New Ager believes that every Ascended Master has become a God in a similar mode as the Source, or The Eternal Mind, or El Shaddai, or God, or I AM, or YHWH, or whatever name is given to the ineffable one, is simply not valid. The Ascended Masters are those who are available for those of us who need help in doing God's work. They may be called on in that sense. And a follower of Christ, or of Buddha, or of Mohammad or of whatever, who feels no need for additional help in order to do God's work, need not call on any of them and they won't appear; for they are not allowed to help unless called upon by the free-will choice of the entity.

Again, the New Ager feels that ascension is a normal progression of the soul as it goes through its eternal development. Because of this, followers of Buddha and of Jesus Christ are equally welcome into the movement and those who believe in "Jesus Christ and him crucified" are not discouraged from that belief. Instead, they are merely opened to the possibility that Jesus preached with a wider vision than that which has been passed on by the decisions of man, however well motivated those decisions may have been. And the mention of Jesus Christ and Buddha above is not meant to be limiting, but only to present these as two examples. Because of this belief on the part of the New Ager, a Christian New Ager will have no problem attending a Christian church or Bible study group in the same week that he is pondering the meaning of an Edgar Cayce work, or the expanded lessons of The Keys of Enoch or the like; and a Buddhist or a Muslim could feel the same way. Although this may turn off some who believe that they know that there is only one way to God whatever that way might be, it is the message of the Unconditional Love preached by the many who have generated the religions of the world, and whose message seems to have been mislaid or forgotten by their followers.

The New Ager views ascension as the eventual right of all Souls, and even of the homes into which those Souls incarnate; for ascension, or rising to higher vibrational frequencies, is an eventual happening not only for the individual, but also for the planet or for any other abode of the Soul. But those who ascend are not always seen by those who have not yet ascended; for since ascension involves movement to a higher frequency of energy, then if a three-dimensional entity were to try to see an ascended person or world through only his physical senses, he probably would not be able to discern separate entities. He would see only an indistinct haze of energy. This is one reason for some of the exercises which New Agers go through; for they help to enhance the senses to the point of discerning those ascended beings for the purpose of sharing in God's work, and of sharing in Unconditional Love.

UNCONDITIONAL LOVE   In the Bible, it is recorded that in answer to the question of what is the great commandment in the law, Jesus replied, ''You shall love the Lord your God with all your heart, and with all your soul, and with all your mind. This is the great and first commandment. And a second is like it, You shall love your neighbor as yourself. On these two commandments depend all the law and the prophets'' [Matthew 22: 37-40]. Loving something with all your heart, soul and mind, and likewise loving your neighbor as yourself is Unconditional Love. It was taught as a complete text by Jesus. It was taught as a partial text by Buddha [love yourself], by Mohammed [love of God, for after all, Islam means "surrender to the will of Allah"], and by others. But unfortunately, Unconditional Love has not often been practiced by the faiths for which it is deemed to be important. Christian love has often been applied only to those of the same faith, as amply demonstrated by the Christian British in Africa and India, the Christian Spanish in Central and South America, and the Christian Fundamentalists in the United States. Another example of sharing love only with those who think alike could be the domineering parent or spouse; for like them, the people of this world have amply demonstrated their capability for saying "Think as I do or I will not love you".

Unconditional Love is, as it implies, love which is given without conditions. It is a desirable goal, albeit a difficult one to achieve. Possibly the most difficult aspect is that of judgment. To call a motorist who is going 75 mph in a 50 mph zone an "idiot" may allow an individual to blow off steam, but it is not unconditional love, for it is making a personal and emotional judgment. That is not love. To tell a child that he is "stupid" because he is not in the top 10% of his class may seem like justifiable motivation to some parents, but it is hardly unconditional love for it implies that the parent will only love the child if he is successful as defined by the parent. It is, therefore, making a judgment. To tell somebody that "my God is superior to your God" is hardly an expression of unconditional love, for it implies that the individual will love the other only if he accepts the "superior" God as his God. It is, therefore, judgmental about the quality of the other person's worship.

Although it is not practiced by all who have been classified as being of the New Age movement, non-judgmental, unconditional love is a belief of the responsible, Spirit-directed members of the New Age movement. Because it will probably take a higher dimension to achieve, it is not an immediate goal, but it is a direction. Because of this direction, the responsible, knowledgeable New Ager will avoid diversions such as mind control and the worship of Satan and will accept and love all others whatever they believe.

INTERACTIONS These five beliefs of the New Age movement interact with each other. A description of these interactions could start with the belief that the Soul gains experience through incarnations. Some of these experiences will create unresolved issues which thus require a reincarnation to resolve. However, the need for this reincarnation is not because of Karma as defined by the Hindu [see Chapter 7]. Instead, it is the Spirit's guidance to the Soul. If this guidance is handled in an acceptable manner, then it will allow the entity to overcome an unresolved issue which is holding back the entity from Ascension into the higher frequencies of Multidimensional existence. And although all of this takes Time, the Soul is speeded along the pathway by the practice of Unconditional Love.

CHAPTER 6   THE EXPERIENCES OF THE PRESENCE OF GOD

The previous Chapter described how the New Ager believes that his Soul makes progress towards oneness with God by gaining and resolving experiences, both when incarnate and when not. It can readily be said that this one belief is central to all that the New Ager feels about himself and his religion. Consequently, it is a belief which requires further definition and understanding.

This Chapter will attempt to generate understanding on this rather complex subject by first examining the concept of Experience in general, and then by examining that special category of experience known as Religious Experience; followed by an examination of two New Age beliefs based on their concept of experience. These beliefs are: [1] the New Age Experience of the Presence of God; and [2] some New Age Experiential beliefs expressed as Articles of Faith.

EXPERIENCE

It is generally accepted that the first approach to understanding experience was that generated during the 18th century by the Classical School of British philosophers represented by John Locke and David Hume. Theirs was a sensual approach in that experience was thought to exist only from reports of the world as perceived by the physical senses. In this way, experiences were distinguished from reasoning or from logic which could be approached without having had any interaction with the physical senses. In this classical approach to understanding experience, the mind was visualized as a wax tablet upon which impressions from the physical senses could be stored. The mind was then considered to be only a passive recipient of the data given to it by the physical senses; and although the mind could compare and relate these data until it achieved a logical understanding, each idea or belief had to be traced back to its origin as received by the physical senses, or else it was not considered to be an experience.

Later, Immanuel Kant and others of the German Idealist School expanded the role of the mind by including interpretation. They developed the thought that there could be experiences not necessarily related to any particular sensual impression by synthesizing new experiences from old experiences. In this way, the mind could review all past physical impressions, interrelate them with a new interpretation, and generate an entirely new experience, one to which no specific originating sensual impression would relate. In this manner, logic, or reason, or even fantasy could become classified as experience. Because of this, experience could be thought of as a many-sided reflection of man's multiple encounters with the world, with other men, and with himself. However, all of these experiences were still thought to relate back to sensual data in some manner, even though the connecting route may be a tenuous one.

In the early part of the 20th century, the Pragmatist School of American philosophers expanded the concept of experiences even further by considering experience to be the medium for disclosing whatever is encountered. In this sense, experience became much broader than anything based merely on the registry of sensual data; for it was seen as a human activity related to the purpose and interest of the one who experiences. It was seen as his interpretation of multiple transactions between himself and his total environment, whether as determined by senses, by logic, by reasoning, by dreaming, or by whatever. William James, who was arguably the most expansive of these philosophers, developed a theory of experience known as ''radical empiricism'', in which experience was not only the experience itself, but also consisted of all relations and connections between that independent experience and other independent experiences. As an extreme example of the application of this theory, a person could ''experience'' a distant and unknown relative by having experienced that person through experiences with the close relatives and friends of that particular person. It is the philosopher's way of saying, ''I feel as if I have known you all my life'' even though it was a first meeting. As an experience, it is a long way from the ''required input of physical sensual data'' needed for an experience by the Classical School.

RELIGIOUS EXPERIENCE

If mankind continued to believe that the only experience available was that based solely on data presented by the five physical senses, then he would be missing a lot of what we presently call ''experiences''. As a few examples, we would not be able to say, ''I have experienced the thrill of seeing a new-born baby and its mother's love''; for although you might see the new baby and its mother, how can you see a ''thrill''? Or we would not be able to say, ''I have experienced the rhapsody of true love''; for again, although we may be able to see the people involved or may even be one of them, how can you physically feel a rhapsody? Or

133

Christian ministers would not be able to ask, "Have you experienced the love of Jesus Christ?" or "Have you experienced Jesus in your life?"; for how can you physically see, hear, smell, taste or touch either "love" or "Jesus"?

And so, because of an expansion in the belief of what an experience can be, we now have the ability to have a "Religious Experience" which fits all of the philosophical definitions of an experience. In modern thinking, religious experiences can include many things such as: wonder at the infinity of the cosmos; a sense of awe in the presence of something holy; feelings of dependence on a divine power; a sense of guilt or anxiety at the possibility of divine judgment; the feeling of peace which accompanies divine forgiveness; and many other experiences which are "obtained without the use of the five physical senses".

"Religious Experience" was not widely used as a technical term until the publication of The Varieties of Religious Experience in 1902 by the previously mentioned William James. However, the interpretation of dogmas, concepts, and doctrines in terms of religious experience goes back to the mystics of 16th century Spain and to the instigators of the Protestant Reformation; for it was the belief in religious experiences which permitted the acceptance on the part of an individual that religion could be an actual and personal force in his daily life. Prior to this, daily religion was primarily a regulator of moral or financial affairs, or was a force to be feared in respect to the eternity of the afterlife. It had few, if any, daily elements of love.

As presently conceived, all religious experiences can be divided into three basic elements: [1] the personal concerns, attitudes, feelings or ideas of the person who has the experience; [2] the religious object disclosed in the experience; and [3] the social problems caused by the sharing of the experience. As one example of how these elements have accompanied a religious experience, as described in Chapter 3, Jesus had concerns and ideas which he expressed; he then disclosed that he was from the Father; and he therefore caused so many social problems that he was crucified. Other religious experiences have had similar histories. One aspect of a religious experience which differs from other experiences is that of its effect on society, particularly on the society of accepted and established religious beliefs, dogmas, or doctrines. Imagine, if you will, what would happen if someone were to say, "I didn't want it to happen to me, but preacher, I now know that Jesus is back. I saw him yesterday and he wanted me to let you know." Can you imagine the response from every Christian church? Or what if someone were to say, "Rabbi, I met Jehovah yesterday and He wanted me to tell you that Jesus really is the Messiah whether you want to believe it or not." Can you imagine the response which that would bring from every Temple? Or what if a Moslem were to say, "I just came from Allah and He told me to let you know that not only are He and Jehovah brother Gods, but your pilgrimage should be to the Wailing Wall in Jerusalem rather than to Mecca." Can you imagine the reaction from every Mosque in Islam? As a contrast to a religious experience, if an architect were to discover a promising new method of construction, his experience would eventually be accepted by others. And the same would be true for an automotive or an airplane designer. The proponents of the new technologies may be shunned for a while by those who had established their reputation on the older technologies, but eventually the new would win out if it were superior to the old. And afterwards, the old timers would congratulate themselves on being smart enough to learn from the experiences of those who had brought them the new thoughts. But that has rarely been true as a result of a religious experience. In that case, if a change occurs, it is often measured in decades, centuries or millennia rather than in weeks, months or years.

All the religious experiences have presented problems to the established religious community, but mysticism has probably caused the deepest rift. It is logical that this should be so, for mysticism is about as far away from sensual verification as any activity could be. By definition, mysticism is that act by which a union is formed with the divine by use of meditation or by other, somewhat similar contemplative techniques. It is one of the core activities in Hinduism and Buddhism, and has appeared, on occasion, in all other religions.

As a religious experience, mysticism has a problem. One of the elements of a religious experience is to share that religious experience with others. This is very difficult for the mystic to do, because words simply are not adequate to transfer the feeling of the mystical experience. Some have tried, but few have succeeded. As an example, the medieval Christian mystic, Meister Eckehart, merely said, "The knower and the known are one. God and I, we are one in knowledge. There is no distinction between us." This obviously is inadequate communication of what he must have felt; but inadequate as it may be, it did thoroughly disturb those in the established church of that day.

Despite disturbances such as this, mysticism has been little more than a pin-prick in the side of Judaism, Christianity or Islam; but even a pin-prick can be felt. As one example, Machiavelli, the 16th century Florentine statesman who brought organization and order to both the state and the church, claimed that the 13th century Christian monastics St. Francis and St. Dominic may have saved the religion, but they almost destroyed the church through their contemplative lives. What he meant was that although a contemplative life may bring that individual closer to Christ, it doesn't help the power of the Church by filling its coffers. In other words, this influential citizen wanted contemplation to be replaced by action.

Many presently believe that the definition of mysticism should be expanded to include "the quest for hidden wisdom" or the search for "the treasure hidden in the center of our souls". In the 20th century, mysticism is undergoing renewed interest, partly because it is now considered to be a religious principle which is available to all men if they would just use it, rather than being available solely to the elite as it once was thought. To support this belief in universality, Aldous Huxley has said that, ''a totally unmystical world would be a world totally blind and insane''. He was meaning that some time should be spent by everyone looking inside to see what they can find, for the mystic truly believes the words of the Bible which say, ''the kingdom of God is within you'' [Luke 17: 21]. In an attempt to look for ''the treasure hidden in the center of the soul'', most mystics will follow the four stages of: [1] purgation of the bodily desires; [2] purification of the will; [3] illumination of the mind; and [4] unification with the divine. As in most religious practices, those who practice mysticism can go to an extreme fringe which may border on lunacy; but within its more mature elements, mysticism is considered by many to be a rational and righteous religious practice. It is thought to approach the ultimate in religious experiences.

NEW AGE EXPERIENCE

To the mature New Ager, the ultimate religious experience is the Presence of God, however that presence is attained. The New Ager believes that the presence can be established by many methods or techniques. One of these is through meditation or contemplation. In this sense, the New Ager could be considered to be a mystic and to engage in mystical practices just as many of the early and medieval Christians did. On the other hand, the New Ager also believes that the Presence of God can be established during his normal daily living for, as described in Chapter 2, the two-way working relationship between the entity and God will help the entity to evolve through experience towards the Presence of God. And in this growth through evolution, the entity will, in a relatively minor way, help the entire cosmos to evolve, thus helping to pull every other entity in the universe closer to the Presence of God.

The New Ager believes that he experiences the presence of God as God performs three functions for him. Those functions are: [1] Guidance; [2] Protection; and [3] Promise.

GUIDANCE is generated by the Spirit working through the individualized Soul to program experiences for a variety of incarnations which the entity needs in order to progress towards oneness with God. Guidance is often needed, but is most powerfully required when the entity reaches a crossroad in a particular incarnation and needs to make an important free-will choice. The choice at the crossroad could be one which would generate for the entity his needed experiences for several subsequent incarnations. Chapter 7 will address in greater detail the specifics of reincarnation and Karma as believed by the New Ager; but for the present, let us assume that an entity has come to a crossroad experience such as that experienced by those who wondered whether or not to participate in the gang rape which Lot proposed for his daughters [Genesis 19:8]. Although most humans would be morally repulsed by such as act, it is not in the moral judgment sense that the entity would feel the Presence of God; for on a non-judgmental basis, such an experience might have been one which Lot needed in order to develop to the mature stage in which he could fulfill his duty to God by helping his uncle, Abraham, to establish a great nation. At such a crossroad time, the entity wants his actions to be Spirit-led rather than Ego-led. At the time of Lot, those who remained at Lot's house were probably Ego-led, for they were then struck blind by the angels of God. We don't know whether some became Spirit-led and left; but we can say that at such a crossroad experience, a sincere New Ager would want to feel Guidance from the Presence of God.

PROTECTION is developed by the Spirit trying to present the entity with Spirit-led experiences by protecting him from those which would be Ego-led. There are techniques which can help call

138

the Spirit into protection, and the New Age practitioner may use these in an attempt to relate totally with Spirit and never with Ego. At times when Spirit gives Protection, the entity will sense the comfort which comes from the Presence of God.

PROMISE is developed by the Spirit communicating to the entity that there is progress being made; that the present incarnation, whatever its pitfalls, was chosen by the Soul for the specific purpose of gaining needed experience; and that there is an afterlife during which all will be understood. When the entity feels the comfort that this Promise rings true, then he can truly feel the Presence of God.

The New Ager is not alone in feeling the Presence of God. There is much literature which records the feeling of that Presence by those of many faiths, particularly when they were defending their Faith. To many, this implies that the particular Faith is not as important as the fact that Faith exists; or again, as Mahatma Ghandi said, ''All religions are true.'' Because of the particulars of birth, of early education, of parental direction, or of individual conversion, many may feel that they have come to know the only ''true'' Faith; but God must have tried in many ways to get all of His children to accept Him. If this is true, then there must be many people whose identification with God [or Faith] might seem strange to others. But if there is some ''truth'' in every Faith which comes from God, isn't it preferable to love and accept a person even though they are of a different Faith? Isn't it better merely to express an opinion about one's Faith, rather than to dictate ''truth'' to another on such an emotion-laden subject? Couldn't an activity which dictates one's Faith and imposes it upon another be defined as Mind Control and therefore be the Absence, rather than the Presence of God?

In order to experience the Presence of God, the mature New Ager may express his opinion, but never his dictation; because

139

he can never dictate while remaining within the non-judgmental aura of Unconditional Love. The mature New Ager believes that Unconditional Love is an indispensable prerequisite for the Presence of God.

ARTICLES OF FAITH

There are no established Articles of Faith for the New Age movement. In addition, since the total New Age religious movement, like the Christian religious movement, encompasses many varieties of faith, then any Articles of Faith which might be developed would differ from similar Articles presented by another New Ager, just as the Articles of Faith of the Presbyterian Church differ from similar Articles published by the Eastern Orthodox Church. Nevertheless, a set of Articles of Faith such as those presented here would be acceptable to many, if not to all, New Agers.

These Articles will be presented in three sections: [1] Entity-related; [2] Cosmos-related; and [3] God-related.

ENTITY-RELATED

As Articles of Faith, the New Ager believes:

1. That each individualized entity is a Child of God and has a spark of God residing within;

2. That this spark of God can grow or evolve throughout eternity so that it can at some point be where God was, but never entirely where He is because God will also grow or evolve via the evolution of His Children;

3. That this spark began as a Soul which was assigned by God to a Group and which was later divided into an individualized entity as that entity evolved;

4. That the Soul is the first structure of life. It evolved

through growth to become an individualized entity. After that, the Soul evolves by accepting and resolving experiences developed in a number of incarnations. An incarnation, or "in-body experience" occurs when the Soul incorporates itself with four other bodies-- physical, mental, emotional and spiritual--within one physical body, thus creating an incarnation or personality. The Soul evolves and grows by accepting from the personality the knowledge of the experiences gained, whether those experiences are physical, men- tal, emotional or spiritual; and whether those experiences are gained during a male or during a female incarnation. In this way, the Soul gains energy from each incarnation. Subsequent to incarnation, personality will get feedback intelligence from the Soul for use in future incarnations;

5. That in order to guide each of these incarnations, the Soul [part of the entity] not only attempts to give immediate feedback to the personality, it also works to strengthen ties with the Spirit [part of God associated with that entity] so that each may help the personality to process the required experiences produc- tively;

6. That there are many helpers who, if called upon by the free-will choice of the personality, will help the Soul and the Spirit strengthen their ties so that the Spirit becomes more and more able to help Soul guide the personality toward the free-will choices which are along the pathway toward a closer relationship between the entity and God; and

7. That optional exercises or techniques are available which can help tie together the workings between the personality, the helpers, the entity's Soul and the entity's Spirit of God so that all are evolving together along the same pathway.

COSMOS-RELATED

As Articles of Faith, the New Ager believes:

1. That he is not alone in the universe, and that the Earth

141

is not the only physical site where an incarnated Soul does, can and will inhabit;

2. That other physical sites do not necessarily exist in the same vibrational frequency as the Earth, so that their incarnated Souls and/or physical structures would not be discernible by our physical senses;

3. That Earth is neither the most highly nor the least highly evolved physical site, and that physical sites both more evolved and less evolved that Earth do exist within God's domain;

4. That evolution may take different courses at different sites so that whereas one site may be more mentally evolved, another may be more physically, emotionally or spiritually evolved;

5. That entities whose vibrational frequencies differ from ours are present on Earth at all times, and that these entities, some of whom are highly evolved helpers, can be called upon for assistance if desired;

6. That if called upon, the help given by those evolved beings who are following the Way will be only that which is needed and which can be used at the present time by the entity for the continued progress of his Soul;

7. That entities can also be multidimensional, meaning that they have evolved to the point of being able to assume the form of any dimension. They could, therefore, assume dimensions of a slow frequency which would be discernible by our physical senses if they were to so choose; or they could assume dimensions of such high frequency that their speed of travel could approach or even exceed that of light. They could, of course, assume dimensions between these extremes; and

8. That despite such evolution, these highly evolved creatures are not the "God before whom there is no other" for they are not evolved to where God is, even though they may have evolved to where God once was. God is not dead, and therefore, He has grown and evolved by their evolution.

GOD-RELATED

As Articles of Faith, the New Ager believes:

1. That there is a God who has existed throughout eternity;
2. That this God caused all things to be created including us;
3. That because we are of His creation, He loves us unconditionally;
4. That throughout eternity, He has had contact with His creations and because of His love, has made available many helpers for their use;
5. That no single helper has been able to do everything that God wished to have done as an eternal answer for those of His creation, and so each helper has done what could be done at that particular time and at that particular stage of evolution for a significant number of God's creations;
6. That some have been able to understand the teachings of each helper at the time of that helper's appearance, but that others have not;
7. That after some period of time, man's practice of the teachings which he has received has tended to become distorted, restrictive and controlling. At this point, those teachings become a crutch for man and become static or crystallized as an expression of God's love and purpose;
8. That God's plan for each and every one of His creatures continues to evolve. It therefore will never become static or crystallized. This, of course, is one of the definitions of eternity;
9. That through eternity, it is God's desire to have all His creations experience and practice Unconditional Love; and
10. That at the end of eternity, all of God's creations will be in His presence.

SUMMARY

The New Ager believes that his eternal Soul needs to experience all that there is in order to find its Way. Once the Way has been found, then the Soul becomes individualized. Once individualized, then the Soul continues to gain and resolve experiences in order to remain on the Way, and to continue to make progress along the Way. Just as many Christians believe that the purpose of life is "to glorify God", many New Agers believe that the purpose of eternity is "to find the Presence of God"; and in so doing, to help all of God's creatures along the Way. To do this, the New Ager tries to experience the Presence of God by experiencing that which Spirit programs for his Soul, by practicing Unconditional Love, and by practicing and living certain Articles of Faith.

CHAPTER 7   CHRISTIAN APOLOGETICS

The term "Christian Apologetics" is probably redundant, for the term "Apologetics" itself is defined as that branch of Christian theology which deals with the proof and defense of Christianity. Consequently, there is no Apologetics other than Christian Apologetics. Nevertheless, it is used in the title of this Chapter to reinforce the fact that the only religious order which seems to feel the need to defend itself against the beliefs of the New Age movement is Christianity in general, and fundamental Christianity in particular, with "fundamental" meaning "the inerrant interpretation of our Bible".

In a previous Chapter, two books were mentioned which practice Apologetics against the New Age [see Chapter 5, references 18 & 19]. Those books, particularly Martin [see reference 3 in Chapter 2], will be used as the outline for this Chapter.

Those who practice Apologetics reject the New Age for a number of reasons, the major ones of which are:

1. All New Age movements are <u>cults</u>;
2. All New Age movements represents false <u>spirits</u> as defined by I John 4: 1-3;
3. All New Age movements are <u>Eastern</u> in philosophy and thus they are non-Christian; and
4. No New Age movement believes in the essential doctrines of the Christian faith as represented by their interpretation of <u>God</u>, <u>Jesus Christ</u>, the <u>Holy Spirit</u>, the <u>Trinity</u>, <u>Mankind</u>, and <u>Salvation</u>.

The underlined words in the paragraph above will become the titles of the various sections of this Chapter, and two additional sections will be added. They are <u>Miscellaneous Beliefs</u> and <u>Summary</u>.

CULTS

A cult is defined by Apologetics as being "a group, religious in nature, which surrounds a leader; or a group of teachings which either denies or misinterprets essential biblical doctrine." It is defined as having the following characteristics:

1. Is headed by a dynamic leader who completely controls the followers;
2. Possesses Scripture which is added to or replaces the Bible as God's Word;
3. Disciplines members by rigid standards from which no deviation is allowed;
4. Has members who move from cult to cult;
5. Has active evangelistic programs which proselytize new members;
6. Generates clergymen by submission rather than by schooling;
7. Has an unstable doctrine which constantly changes;
8. Communicates with God, but with new revelations which replace the old;

9. Has an exclusivity on truth; and
10. Applies new meanings to familiar words.

The Apologetics believe that cults are growing in number because:

1. Christianity has permitted liberalism to creep in with liberalism meaning ''as understanding develops, beliefs change rather than remaining unchanged as they do when based on the inerrant truth of the Bible'';
2. There is a desire on the part of individuals in the U.S. to be isolated from society with society being defined as the ''togetherness created by true love and devotion that is kept together by the supernatural bonds of the Holy Spirit, as in true Christianity'';
3. The U.S. is becoming a society which promotes the self-deification of the individual;
4. Our young people have become rebellious and disillusioned with their parent's traditional values, especially as one traditional value, religious belief, has become more of a personal matter than a family issue; and
5. The U.S. has recently been permitting a lot of Eastern thought to enter into our national consciousness.

The Apologetics propose to combat these cults by ''offering a better alternative--the true Christ and true Christianity''.[22]

In answer to these charges, many New Agers would reply:

1. That they do not belong to any cult;
2. That they do not feel controlled in any way;
3. That the Bible is as meaningful to them as it is to any Christian;
4. That new information and understanding is being developed every day in all fields of endeavor, including religious understanding; and

147

5. That no one or no belief has an exclusivity on truth.

In respect to the Bible issue, the New Ager feels that as new scholarly information becomes developed by the discovery of authentic ancient texts, or by the use of newly accepted definitions of old words, then the previously ''inerrant acceptance of the Bible'' needs to be reconsidered and reunderstood. Of the two Apologetic books cited, one uses the New International Version of the Bible and the other uses the King James Version for its scriptural references and quotations. Neither of these Versions has the preponderance of acceptance which is represented by the Revised Standard Version, and each has significant differences of word usage in certain key passages. Those differences in scriptural wording are selectively used within each book as a mechanism to present its particular case. Since the Revised Standard Version seems to have more mainline support as the generally accepted Bible of the English language, it will be used as the reference for this book.

In respect to developing a change in some beliefs as knowledge develops and certain new concepts become accepted, the New Ager feels that any time a religion gets frozen into a particular set of beliefs in the face of new information or thought, then that religion will stagnate and die no matter how much it has previously been accepted as being true. As a few examples, can you imagine what Christianity would be like today if the following ideas or movements had been ignored: [1] the idea of printing the Bible so that all could read it instead of only the Priests; [2] the concept of letting everybody be allowed to pray directly to God rather than through a Saint; [3] the entire concept of the Reformation; or [4] the concept of having a separation of Church and State? To have neglected these and many other progressive movements would have been to cause Christianity to stagnate as it did in the medieval days of state and Papal control; and yet, every one of these ideas was greeted by the established religious order of its day as being heretical. If they could have had their way, the Apologetics of that day would have defended their form of Christianity against every one of these ideas or concepts. If they had been successful, then today, Jesus Christ would be hidden behind the inerrant dictates of a Papal overlord, just as he was some 1,000 years ago. Today, if the Apologetics would have their way, he would remain hidden behind the words of a book which was translated in 1611. Those who wrote the King James Version [KJV] in 1611 did the best they could in view of the tools they had to work with; but today, most scholars feel that the KJV contains grave defects in content and in the modern meaning of the words which were used. Anyone who calls the KJV inerrant, is neglecting almost 400 years worth of scholarly progress. Many New Agers, like many practicing Christians, adore the poetic style of the KJV; but they will argue with the dogmas contained therein. This issue will be addressed in subsequent portions of this Chapter.

SPIRIT

According to the Apologetics, that which comes from Spirit must pass a test as to whether or not it is from a true or a false Spirit. They believe that the test for a true Spirit is presented in verses such as I John 4:1-3 which says:

"Beloved, do not believe every spirit, but test the spirits to see whether they are of God; for many false prophets have gone out into the world. By this you know the Spirit of God: every spirit which confesses that Jesus Christ has come in the flesh is of God, and every spirit which does not confess Jesus is not of God. This is the spirit of antichrist, of which you have heard that it was coming, and now it is in the world already."[23]

The first prophecy of the coming of the Christ is presented in Isaiah 7:14 which says, "Therefore the Lord himself will give you a sign. Behold, a young woman shall conceive and bear a son, and shall call his name Immanuel [which means 'God is with us']''. There is no doubt that many, if not most, New Agers believe that Jesus Christ was indeed made as ''God is with us''. There is no denial of Christ in the New Age movement. There is merely the denial that he represents the only time that there has been a God with us. This particular doctrine [*i.e.* that which is taught] or dogma [*i.e.* that which is proclaimed to be true by a religious sect] will be examined further in the later section of this Chapter entitled ''Jesus Christ''. For the present, let it suffice to say that although some may decide to follow a leader who would not pass the test of 1 John 4:1-3, a significant part of the New Age movement cannot be judged false by this test, for the biblical reference cited merely has as its test the acceptance of the fact that when Jesus Christ was on this physical plane, he was indeed Immanuel, or ''God is with us'' Most New Agers believe that.

EASTERN

The Apologetics believe that all New Age religion should be rejected out-of-hand, because it is Eastern in its philosophy and in its religious practices or beliefs. As mentioned in Chapter 5, the New Ager believes that the roots of Christianity are based in Eastern thoughts and practices, but that Christianity then became Westernized by the initial activities and practices of Rome which were later augmented by the thoughts, activities and practices of the Reformation. It is not the purpose of this Chapter to embellish that issue, for it is one which could go on forever; and the final resolution would be based on the differing beliefs of each party, with the Apologetics stating that Christianity has nothing to do with the East and the New Ager stating that its basic roots are there Instead of that somewhat inane debate, this Chapter will try to address the major concerns which the Apologetics have about the Eastern beliefs of the New Age religion: that it uses <u>Mantras</u>; that it believes in <u>Reincarnation</u> and <u>Karma</u>; and that its God is <u>Pantheistic</u>.

MANTRA is by definition a practice of Hinduism. It is a sacred formula believed to embody the divinity invoked and to possess magical power. It is used in prayer and meditation. To the Hindu, the use of a Mantra is a sacred thing; and although Hindus have very little in the way of organized dogmas, the use of a Mantra is about as close to being a Hindu dogma as anything could be. It is almost one of their laws or commandments. It is used during meditation to bring calm so that the personality may come more nearly into the mystical presence of God than it would if the physical body of the personality were allowed to interfere with its jumble of uncalmed thoughts. In addition, in the practice of using a Mantra, the Hindu does call upon the divinity whose presence is felt to reside in power of the Mantra. Many times, the Hindu will have a special Mantra prepared for and given to him for his personal use. To a Hindu, the Mantra is a mystical, if not a magical, thing.

Some, but not all, members of the New Age movement believe in the power of the Mantra. Some, but not all, members of the New Age movement will use the Mantra as a calming influence in the initial stages of meditation in a manner somewhat similar to a Roman Catholic using the Rosary. Some, but not all, members of the New Age movement will chant during meditation or worship services.

Most members of the New Age movement do not accept that a God resides within the Mantra, anymore than a Christian will believe that his God resides in the use of the Rosary or in the use of the phrase, ''Our Father who art in Heaven...''. Most members of the New Age movement who chant, do not believe that their chanting has any more significance than the Gregorian chants used in some Christian churches. Most members of the New Age movement accept the Mantra as an aid for worship, as a ''crutch'' for helping to remove the barriers between the individual and his God in the same sense as a Roman Catholic will use the beads as he repeats the "Hail Mary" or the "Pater Noster". The mantras used by the major part of the New Age movement are no more Hinduism than the repeated use of a "Hail Mary" is; and the chants used by the major portion of the New Age movement are no more Hinduism than then the singing of "The Old Rugged Cross" or "Peace in the Valley" is. Each is a form of calming presence with which the religious person is familiar and which can therefore lead to a more meaningful prayer [i.e. talking to God] or meditation [i.e. listening to God]. And meditation is as much a Christian practice as it is Hinduistic. As one example, on the entrance to the Chapel of the largest Presbyterian Church in the United States are the words, "Come in and Meditate".

The Mantra had its birth many, many years ago. It is part of the Eastern-New Age heritage. The daily life rules and ordinances found in Exodus, Chapters 21-23 or the dietary laws found in Deuteronomy all had their birth many, many years ago, They are a part of the Judeo-Christian heritage. A Christian can practice his religion today without immersing himself in all of the practices upon which his religion is historically based. In a similar manner, a New Ager can practice his religion today without immersing himself in all of its heritage.

Some who belong to the New Age movement are deep into their Eastern heritage as represented by the use of a Mantra; many are not. All who come with the attitude of Unconditional Love are accepted.

REINCARNATION is different than the Mantra, for although some New Agers accept help from the Mantra, others do not; but as mentioned in Chapter 6, the New Ager has Reincarnation as an Article of Faith. His belief in reincarnation is so universal and strong, that he has a difficult time understanding why all do not accept it as a belief. And Reincarnation is a belief. As such it may or may not be factual. Proving Reincarnation as a fact is as difficult

152

as proving Heaven as a fact; for since the only proof for either involves dying, it is difficult to run a controlled experiment.

Despite this difficulty, the basis for believing in Reincarnation is becoming so strong that many are starting to state that the basis is factual. The factual base is not of a type that would be acceptable to a roomful of disinterested scientists, but it is of a type that would make many of those disinterested scientists start to think. As a few examples of the voluminous literature being published on reincarnation, both Life Before Life and Life Beyond Life were written by authors, each of whom had gone through the rigorous testing required to earn a Ph.D.; and both the Case for Reincarnation and Reincarnation: A Biblical Doctrine? make for compelling reading. [24] The latter book was written by a graduate of the seminary at Moody Bible Institute who has a Doctor of Divinity degree. It uses more than 200 scriptures from the Bible to support the belief in reincarnation.

Furthermore, although the belief in reincarnation may have started in the East, it is no longer solely an Eastern belief. In the book, Reincarnation, An East-West Anthology, the authors list over 200 pages of references on reincarnation from Western authors and thinkers, including Dante, Michelangelo, Sir Francis Bacon, David Hume, Thomas Carlyle, Bertrand Russell, John Milton, Samuel Coleridge, Rudyard Kipling, Charles Dickens, Arthur Conan Doyle, Isaac D'Israeli, Lloyd George, Frederick the Great, Immanuel Kant, Goethe, Albert Schweitzer, Voltaire, Napoleon Bonaparte, Balzac, Victor Hugo, Tolstoy, Dostoevsky, Benjamin Franklin, Thomas Paine, Ralph Waldo Emerson, Henry David Thoreau, Henry Wadsworth Longfellow, Oliver Wendell Holmes, Walt Whitman, Mark Twain, J. D. Salinger, Henry Ford, William Randolf Hearst, Henry Houdini, Charles Lindbergh, Thomas Edison, William James, Carl Jung, Charles Darwin, Albert Einstein, and many, many others.

Finally, it should be understood that the major Christian denial of reincarnation was established during the Fifth Ecumenical Council at the Second Council of Constantinople in AD 553. At this Council, many things were established which would make those who believed in them an anathema, or one who was to be excommunicated. Among the more curious of things which issued from this council were; [1] if one thought that the soul of the Lord pre-existed and was united with God before the Incarnation of the Virgin; or [2] if one thought that his resurrection would be in any form other than in his presently existing body, then the individual would be subject to excommunication. It is obvious to anyone who has studied any Protestant form of religion that the first of these beliefs is substantiated by the first five verses of the Gospel according to John; and that the second is based on a definition of "body" which is disputed by many. It should also be noted that this council: [1] was called by the Byzantine Emperor Justinian rather than by the Pope at that time, Pope Vigilius; [2] was not attended by the Pope even though he was in Constantinople at the time; and [3] was called by Justinian solely because of the feud between the Eastern and the Western branches of the Church. In addition, it was attended solely by Eastern and African bishops with no one from Rome attending, and had as its major purpose the condemnation of the teachings of Origen. The fact that Origen had a high standing in the Church of that day has been attested to by St. Jerome and St. Gregory, as had the fact that Emperor Justinian had political feuds with both Origen and the Western branch of the Church. Today, many Catholic scholars consider Origen to be "the most prominent of all the Church Fathers with the possible exception of Augustine". In addition, at one time St. Jerome considered Origen as "the greatest teacher of the Church after the Apostles", and St. Gregory of Nyssa considered Origen to be "the prince of Christian learning in the third century".[25]

The major problem which Justinian had with the teachings of Origen concerned the teaching of the pre-existence of the soul, a major tenet for a belief in reincarnation. In the Catholic Encyclopedia[26] there is raised a fairly strong disclaimer that the Church at Rome ever took any part in the condemnation of Origen. However, despite this disclaimer, the Catholic Church has continued to exclude from its creed the major teaching of Origen, that of the pre-existence of the soul. Such a creed is necessary if one is to believe in reincarnation.

In reviewing this history, it seems somewhat ironic that although reincarnation is presently considered to be an Eastern belief, it was the Eastern branch of the Christian Church which condemned it and the Western branch which took no activity in its condemnation. It is also somewhat ironic that Origen, a church father who is so highly respected by history and whose teachings in the early church are so highly rated, would today have his teachings excluded primarily because of a "territorial prerogative" feud with Justinian, an Emperor whose theological interventions are not respected by history. As two examples of the latter, some of Justinian's edicts concerning the "body of Christ" were declared heretical by the Church in Rome: and, unlike Jesus Christ who accepted the Samaritans, Justinian passed edicts which forbade them to teach any Christian theology.

But the principle justification for the presentation on reincarnation given in this book does not relate to how the pre-existence of the soul became condemned as Christian teaching by a political feud in the 6th century church; instead it relates to what the Judeo-Christian heritage in general, and the Bible in particular, have to say about reincarnation.

First, it should be noted that the word "reincarnation" does not appear in the Bible; but then neither does the word "trinity". Those who believe in the inerrant teachings of the Bible accept the Trinity as both a doctrine and a dogma, not because it is presented as such in the Bible, but because the single word

"Trinity" conveys a truth which is inferred in the Bible even though the Bible uses many words other than "trinity" to express belief in that Christian doctrine. The New Ager feels exactly the same about the word "reincarnation"; that although the word itself is not used as such in the Bible, many other words are used to express belief in that New Age doctrine.

This book will not present all the scriptural references which could relate to reincarnation. As previously mentioned, another book has presented over 200 scriptures which support the belief in reincarnation. Nevertheless, the following four from the New Testament seem particularly pertinent[27]:

1. "And Jesus went on with his disciples, to the villages of Caesarea Phillippi; and on the way he asked his disciples, 'Who do men say that I am?' And they told him, 'John the Baptist; and others say Elijah; and others one of the prophets.' " [Mark 8: 27-8]

2. "And as they were coming down the mountain, Jesus commanded them, 'Tell no one the vision, until the Son of man is raised from the dead.' And the disciples asked him, 'Then why do the scribes say that first Elijah must come?' He replied, 'Elijah does come, and he is to restore all things; but I tell you that Elijah has already come, and they did not know him, but did to him whatever they pleased.' " [Matt. 17: 9-12]

3. "For all the prophets and the law prophesied until John; and if you are willing to accept it, he is Elijah who is to come. He who has ears to hear, let him hear." [Matt. 11: 13-15]

4. "There was a man sent from God whose name was John" [John 1: 6]

The first reference is almost self-explanatory, for how could people say that you "are" one of the prophets if there were not a current belief in reincarnation which Jesus did not dispute. The second reference refers to John the Baptist who had already been beheaded and whom Jesus had already identified as Elijah in the third reference. How could Jesus say ''he is Elijah'' unless he was agreeing with the then current belief that reincarnation existed [see next paragraph]. The fourth reference was used by Origen to substantiate the pre-existence of the soul in that John the Baptist's soul must have existed before his terrestrial body, for, ''And if the Catholic opinion hold good concerning the soul, as not propagated with the body, but existing previously and for various reasons clothed in flesh and blood this expression 'Sent from God' will no longer seem extraordinary as applied to John.'' The New Ager would applaud Origen's statement, but add that if it ''no longer will seem so extraordinary as applied to John'', then it will no longer seem so extraordinary when applied to any individualized entity, for John, extraordinary as he was in fulfilling God's purpose for him, has never been considered anything other than an ordinary person doing what he was sent here to do. That is what the New Ager feels about himself--that he is an ordinary person doing what he was sent here to do. And the sender is the Soul working with Spirit which is of God.

As a part of examining the Judeo-Christian heritage for beliefs about reincarnation, it would be of great interest to understand further the prevailing opinions among the leading religious elements of Jesus' time. As described in Chapter 3, those elements were the Pharisees which were the largest, the Essenes which were next largest, and the priestly Sadducees which were the smallest of the three. According to the Jewish historian Flavius Josephus, the doctrine of the Sadducees was that the soul died with the body. To the Sadducees, there was no afterlife, even one such as Christians would accept. But both the Pharisees and the Essenes believed in rebirth. As to the Pharisees, Josephus states, ''The Pharisees believe that souls have an immortal vigour in them and that the virtuous shall have power to revive and live again: on account of

157

which doctrines they are able greatly to persuade the body of the people.'' In respect to the Essenes, Josephus states, '' They smiled in their very pains and laughed to scorn those who inflicted torments upon them, and resigned up their souls with great alacrity, as expecting to receive them again.''[28] It seems fair to state that Jesus, who was a man of the people rather than of the priestly rulers, would have had views more nearly like those of the Pharisees and the Essenes than those of the Sadducees, especially since Jesus had such strong convictions about the afterlife. In addition, since Jesus did not refute his followers when they spoke of the concept of reincarnation [see the first three New Testament quotations given above], then it would seem again that he agreed with the prevailing opinion of the time. That opinion was that there was a rebirth, or what we would now call ''reincarnation''.

In addition, many early Christian writers and teachers speak strongly about the pre-existence of the soul which is one of the elements required for reincarnation. Among these were Origen, St. Jerome, St. Augustine, St. Clement, and St. Gregory who said, ''It is absolutely necessary that the soul should be healed and purified, and if this does not take place during its life on earth, it must be accomplished in future lives.''[29]

Finally, in an authoritative nationwide poll conducted in 1987 by Chicago's National Opinion Research Council, more than 25% of the people contacted expressed their belief in reincarnation.[30] If this were to hold on a nationwide basis as most well-conducted polls are supposed to do, this would mean that more than 65 million people in the U.S. believe in reincarnation. As such, they could be considered to be a part of the New Age movement. Only a very few of these people belong to any ''cult'' of the type mentioned in the two books by the Apologetics.

The Apologetics do not accept reincarnation as a belief; the New Agers do. Any debate over belief is inane in that each has the right to believe as he chooses and to interpret biblical passages as he chooses. Within the practice of acceptance-rejection [see Introduction], many beliefs can be acceptable without compromising the belief in "Jesus Christ and him crucified" which is the basis of Biblical Christianity whatever man may have later added in doctrinal or dogmatic concerns such as Trinity, Mankind, Salvation and the like.

KARMA, like Mantra, is by definition a Hinduistic belief. It is a belief which is also accepted by Buddhists. It is therefore Eastern in its origin. It is presently defined as the sum and the consequences of a person's actions during the successive phases of his existence, regarded as determining his destiny. In a non-theological sense, it is defined as fate or destiny. Unlike Mantra, Karma, in the sense used by the New Ager, is not optional. It, like reincarnation with which it networks, is an Article of Faith.

But the way in which the New Ager thinks of Karma is different than the way that a Hindu views it. To the Hindu, Karma is a law which determines life, for his rebirth is based upon his moral behavior in a previous phase of existence. In this way, the caste system has been developed out of which an individual cannot raise himself. Thus, this life, which is a burden, must be lived through with no hope of atonement, restitution or experience other than to get out of this transient existence and to enter into another cycle of birth-rebirth until all past moral debts have been excised by non-active lives of meditation. When that happens, then nirvana [extinction of all passion] is reached.

The New Ager accepts Karma as the purpose for his present existence, but in this case, Karma is defined as the experiences needed to continue progress along the Way. The need for some of those experiences may come from unresolved past experiences which need to be resolved. Some of these past experiences may have been morally acceptable; others not. In this

159

way, the Karma of the New Ager is not always negative as is that of the Hindu; it is merely that which must be experienced. In addition, Karma to the New Ager is not in the direction of the extinction of all passions by continued lives of non-activity. Instead, the New Ager needs to be active and passionate in the sense of knowing himself, believing in himself and knowing that he is on the pathway of oneness with God. This pathway is not a passive one to the New Ager.

It is the belief of the New Ager that the goals of Karma originally established with reverence and belief by the Hindu became subjugated to a political purpose when the Aryans from the North conquered major parts of India at about the same time that the biblical Exodus occurred. At this point, the conquerors wanted a method to control and defuse the passions of the conquered people. What better way than to convince them that they were inferior by assigning them to a caste for life; one out of which they could not rise and into which they were assigned because of something that they previously had done whether they remembered it or not. As a consequence of all of this, the New Age belief in Karma is quite different from the Hindu belief. One leads to freedom; the other to control. One becomes the entity using his Soul in conjunction with Spirit to make progress; the other becomes an entity justifying his present existence. And although each practice can make its practitioner feel that it is a worthwhile endeavor, it will be for significantly different reasons.

There is an additional belief in Karma which is accepted by the New Ager. That is the belief that the collective consciousness of the entire Earth population can have Karma [*i.e.* need for specific experiences] which can be eliminated by the hierarchy if progress is being made by a sufficient number of people working on the behalf of the collective consciousness. The New Ager believes that such an elimination of the need for Karma could change the plans which the hierarchy might have for the future direction of the planetary consciousness. The New Ager further believes that such a change in plans did occur at the time of the harmonic convergence. Enough people had awakened and participated that the original catastrophic plans for Earth were changed and a significant amount of Karma [some say more than 50%] was eliminated from the planetary consciousness. In this instance, the hierarchy operated today just as it did in the days of Sodom and Gomorrah where if only a few righteous people had been found, the cities would have been saved. Unfortunately, not enough were found, so the destruction came, but only after the few righteous ones were removed [Genesis 18:16 through 19:29].

The experiences which make progress by resolving unresolved experiences is an important part of the New Age belief. Although such experiences are called by the name Karma for reasons of communication and understanding, it is not the same as the Karma used in the totally Eastern religions. And although the Apologetics have stated that the doctrine of karma is not to be found in the Bible, in the New Ager's mind, when Paul wrote, "Do not be deceived; God is not mocked, for whatever a man sows, that he will also reap" [Gal. 6:7] he was making one of the strongest statements on Karma that has ever been recorded.

PANTHEISM is defined as the doctrine identifying the Deity with the various forces and workings of nature. As a word, it is of Western rather than Eastern origin. It was first used to describe the philosophy of John Toland in the early 18th century. It has since been retrospectively applied to many aspects of both Eastern and Western philosophy. In retrospect, the earliest, thoroughly defined pantheistic system was proposed by the Jewish rationalist, Benedict Spinoza, in the mid-17th century. Spinoza insisted that since God was infinite, then God could not be absent from the world since therefore God plus world would be greater than God. Therefore the world must exist as a part of God. As theology, pantheism stresses the all-inclusiveness of God as contrasted with the separateness of God emphasized in many Theisms.

Christian theologians have traditionally rejected Pantheism because it tends to make the Creator and His creations indistinct from each other, to make God impersonal, to make God immanent [*i.e.* existing within] rather than transcendent [*i.e.* existing above and independent of the material universe] and to exclude human and Divine freedom.

Pantheism is generally monistic, meaning that there is a sense of the unity of the world and the divine, and that there is the probability of a personal union with God; whereas Theism is generally dualistic, meaning that God is separate from the world just as the human mind is separate from the body. Because God and the world are one in Pantheism, then it is generally considered that man is an absolutely fated part of the world [*i.e.* his destiny has already been determined] and thus human freedom is an illusion; whereas in Theism, man has many degrees of freedom to the point of being almost absolutely free.

It is generally considered that there are at least seven distinct types of Pantheism, ranging all the way from Hylozoistic pantheism [the divine is the basic element of the world] to Emanationistic pantheism [God is absolute in all respects, remote from the world and transcendent over it]. With such a wide range of definitions of God, almost anything could be called pantheistic, and since ''pan'' refers to ''all'' and ''theo'' refers to God, then anyone who believes that ''God is All'' must, by derivation of the word, be considered to be a pantheist. However, the Apologetics will state that no monistic God can be a Biblical God for three reasons; [1] since God created the heavens and the earth, then those things are not eternal whereas God is. Therefore the Creator and the created must be separate and distinct; [2] that although God is omnipresent [i.e. present everywhere] it does not mean that He is in anything, but only that He pays attention to everything; and [3] that God is defined as being a personal God, meaning that He exists as the person who was the "I AM WHO I AM" of Exodus 3:14. In this definition, they do not mean that God is a personal God in the sense that an individual could have a personal relationship with Him; they mean that He is a personal God in the sense of being a distinct person and not a nebulous form of energy or the like.

To the New Ager, it seems that one problem with religious analysis is the attempt to put everything into a specific category or to use, if you will, an "acid test" to determine who or what an individual is. This is sort of like putting labels on a politician by giving him an "acid test" to determine who or what he is. Often the person gets defined not so much by who or what he is, but by the prejudices of the one applying the "acid test". To the New Ager, calling the New Age movement a pantheistic movement is an example of such an "acid test".

The New Ager believes that God created, for example, a tree. This does not mean that the tree is to be worshipped as a God, for the tree is not God; nevertheless the tree can be honored as containing a spark of God or as being evidence of the greatness of God for as it says in Romans 1: 19-20, "For what can be known about God is plain to them, because God has shown it to them. Ever since the creation of the world his invisible nature, namely, his eternal power and deity, has been clearly perceived in the things that have been made." What this means is that the power and deity [*i.e.* Godlike nature] of God can be seen in a tree; and as such, the tree should be honored. And since God is omnipresent [*i.e.* in all places], and since it becomes very difficult to pay attention to things without being a part of them, then how can an omnipresent God who is doing His part of the job be anything other than a part of the things He created. Granted, He is more than those things for He is eternal; but does that keep Him from being a part of them any more than an earthly father is a part of his son even though they are two distinct human beings? And why can't a personal God be personal

163

in the sense that He can establish a personal relationship as well as being personal in the sense of being a "person"?

There was an awfully lot of "the acid test" connotation associated with the questions asked by the House Committee on Unamerican Activities in the late 1940s and early 1950s when they asked, "Are you now or have you ever been a member of the Communist Party or do you know anyone who has?" It is sort of like "Are you now or have you ever been a Pantheist or do you know anyone who has?"

There is a lot in the Pantheistic doctrines which appeal to the New Ager, some of which seems to be like Christianity was before the doctrines and dogmas got so set.

GOD

The Apostles' Creed is considered by most Christians and their Church to be a powerful statement of faith. It is used in the Roman Catholic, Anglican, and many Protestant churches although it is not used in the Eastern Orthodox Churches. According to tradition, it was composed by the 12 Apostles; but this is probably only a tradition. It is most probable that the Creed was derived from early interrogations of those who were to be baptized, at which time the bishop would ask, "Do you believe in God, the Father almighty?" and other such questions which were meant to determine if the Christian were faithful. After some period of time, these questions of belief were assembled into what is now called the Apostles' Creed. It was accepted as the definitive statement of faith by the Western Catholic Church during the time that Innocent III was pope [about 1200 AD].

Because of its general acceptance as a definitive statement of faith by most Christians, this Chapter will use the Apostles' Creed as the basis for defining some of the various topics which the

Apologetics have used to differentiate between Christianity and the New Age religion.

The complete Apostles' Creed as used in the Presbyterian church is as follows:

"I BELIEVE in God the Father Almighty, Maker of heaven and earth; And in Jesus Christ His only Son our Lord; who was conceived by the Holy Ghost, born of the Virgin Mary, suffered under Pontius Pilate, was crucified, dead and buried; He descended into hell*; the third day He rose again from the dead; He ascended into heaven, and sitteth on the right hand of God the Father Almighty; from thence He shall come to judge the quick and the dead.

I believe in the Holy Ghost; the holy Catholic Church; the communion of saints; the forgiveness of sins; the resurrection of the body; and the life everlasting. AMEN.''

* Some churches omit this.

The complete Apostles' Creed as used in the Roman Catholic Church presents only three minor differences as:

1. He was conceived by the power of the Holy Spirit and born of the Virgin Mary;
2. He descended to the dead; and
3. He shall come again to judge the living and the dead.

The remainder is essentially identical.

In this declaration of faith, the Christians' view of God is as "the Father Almighty, Maker of heaven and earth". With one minor exception, the New Ager has no problem with this as a definition of God. The New Ager believes that God [by whatever name] made [or caused to be made which is the same thing] heaven and earth and all else that exists. The only exception which the New Ager would make is in the use of the term "Father" which, in the

Creed is capitalized as if it were a title rather than a sexual description. The New Ager believes that the world in the early Christian era was a very male-driven world, and as a consequence, all positive attributes were generally attributed to the male. The female was rarely mentioned.

The New Ager believes that God has no sexual duality, *i.e.* that "He" is a balance of the sexual entities. This means that sex has no meaning when referring to God: that "He" is either sexless, or that all sexes are present, which is the same thing. If the Christian accepts that "Father God" is a title rather than a sexual connotation, then the New Ager has no problem with the Christian definition of God. If, however, the Apologetics truly believe and defend that "God is a male and that is the way it is", then the New Ager would suggest that they take a poll of Christendom. One of the sad elements of a major part of the Judeo-Christian heritage has been its rejection of the female as a fully qualified representative of God. She is accepted as such in the New Age movement.

JESUS CHRIST

The Apostles' Creed says eight major things about Jesus Christ as follows:

1. [he was] His only Son our Lord;
2. [he was] Conceived by the Holy Ghost [or by the power of the Holy Spirit];
3. [he was] Born of the Virgin Mary;
4, [he] Suffered under Pontius Pilate;
5. [he] Was crucified, dead and buried;
6. He rose again from the dead
7. He ascended into heaven
8. He shall come to judge the quick [or the living] and the dead.

Because some of the major differences between the Apologetics and the New Agers relate to the person and the body of beliefs about Jesus Christ, this section will present a discussion on each of these eight topics or characteristics in the same order as presented in the Apostles' Creed. The major subjects will be items 1, 3, and 7; i.e. the only Son; born of Virgin Mary; and ascended into heaven. The others will require only minor amounts of discussion.

1. HIS ONLY SON OUR LORD Although there are some exceptions, most New Agers have absolutely no problem with accepting the belief that Jesus Christ was the Son of God. In addition, many New Agers accept Jesus Christ as their Lord and as the one through whom progress toward oneness with God [one of the conceptual definitions of salvation] will be sought and achieved. However, much as they may believe in his divinity and special mission among us, almost no New Ager believes that Jesus Christ was the only Son of God. In addition, the mature New Ager does not believe that the concept of Jesus Christ as being the only Son of God is biblical, but instead has been developed by man to make Jesus Christ seem to be even more special than he was in the scriptures. These thoughts obviously differ greatly from the thoughts of the Apologetics on the same subject. This difference will be the major part of this particular discussion.

In the scriptures, Jesus was known by several descriptive titles. The description which Jesus most often had of himself was "Son of man". This title is used fourteen times in Mark, the first gospel to be written, and thirty-one times in the longer gospel of Matthew. In contrast, the term "Messiah" [or its Greek equivalent, "Christ"] is used only six times in the text of Mark's gospel and is used only once by Jesus in referring to himself at which point he immediately goes on to refer to the messiah as the "Son of man" [Mark 14: 61-2]. However, despite this reticence to call himself the messiah [or Christ, or Son of David], on four instances when others called him this name or title, he did not refute it. These occurrences are recorded in Matthew 16:16; Mark 5:19; Mark 10:48; and the afore-mentioned Mark 14:61. But the major point to be understood is that when talking about himself, Jesus most often called himself "Son of man" rather than messiah, Christ or Son of God.

The Appendix, which starts on page 231, presents the fifty-nine times in the New Testament that Jesus is called the "Son of God" or a similar phrase. Thirty-five of these are in the gospels. In only five of these gospel references does Jesus refer to himself as the "Son of God" or a corresponding title. Of these five, two are in the early written, historic gospels. They are Matthew 11:27 and the corresponding Luke 10:22 [references 2 and 21 in the Appendix]. In these powerful statements, Jesus leaves no doubt that he enjoys an unusual Father-Son relationship with God about which there can be no misunderstanding. But the important point to be made is that in only one historical instance in the first three gospels does Jesus refer to himself as having such a relationship with God.

The other three times that Jesus called himself a title such as "Son of God" are in John. They are references 30, 31, and 33 in the Appendix. The gospel of John is different than the other three gospels for a number of reasons. First, although the author and the exact date of its writing are not known, it was probably written much later than the others. Secondly, it may have been written in two parts, the first [Chapters 1-20] directed at the Jews in Jerusalem and the last Chapter [Chapter 21] added to influence an audience in a Greek city, possibly Ephesus. Third, it has many theological elements which present a defense of the faith in it; whereas the first three are written more from the viewpoint of a historical reporter. In fact, this defense of the faith is so obvious, that B.H. Streeter in his monumental work on the gospels wrote that the gospel of John derives "not from the original authorities, but from the vivid picture ...[of the author's] imagination on the basis of contemporary apologetics.''[31] In other words, the gospel which says that Jesus called himself ''Son of God'' three times as much as the other three gospels combined, was written by one who was defending a faith that was based on Jesus Christ being the Son of God. For some time, Biblical scholars doubted the credibility of the gospel according to John. Later, the discovery of second century writings from archaeological excavations have reinstated John's gospel as a credible telling of the life and teachings of Jesus, albeit one written more in defense of the faith than as a presentation of historical information.

But even if all four gospels are accepted as factual, unvarnished truth, none of it refers to Jesus as the only Son of God, meaning that God has no other sons. An examination of the Appendix will show that there are many statements which has God saying ''my Son''; but this does not imply that there is only one son any more than a father of six sons would when he would introduce one of them by saying, ''This is my son''. It is an introduction, not a statement of singularity. Other statements in the Appendix have others describing Jesus as ''the Son of God''; but again this does not imply a solitary son any more than if someone were to introduce Charlie as ''the son of Henry''. The word ''the'' is a part of a title or an introduction. It does not necessarily mean that Charlie is an only son. It could be used as an introduction even if Henry had six other sons.

And besides that, most languages do not have a definite article such as the English ''the'' and an indefinite article such as the English ''a''. Instead, they use the same article to represent either. The New Testament was originally written in Greek; and the King James Version of the English Bible owes much of its origin either to the Tyndale Bible which was translated from Greek [see Chapter 3] or the Vulgate Bible which was written in Latin and had been translated from Greek. The Greek language has a word for ''the'' but no word for ''a''. Therefore, anything written in Greek would be expressed by using the definite article whether it was definitive or not. Latin, on the other hand, has <u>no</u> word for ''the'' and only occasionally uses a word for ''a''. Therefore, anything written in Latin would be expressed by using the indefinite article. As a consequence of all of this, any Bible translated into English from either Greek or Latin [as all of them were] would be totally unable to differentiate between ''the Son'' and ''a Son'' except at the whim of the translator; and anyone who tries to make such a distinction based on the English differentiation between ''the'' and ''a'' is indeed on an unstable foundation.

A further examination of the Appendix will show that the only times the words ''only Son'' are used in the gospels are in references 23, 24 and 27. All three references are from John. There is only one reference in the New Testament outside of the gospels which uses the term ''only Son''. That is reference 55 which is I John 4:9. For a number of reasons, Biblical scholars believe [but are not certain] that the gospel of John and the letters of John were written by the same man; but that this man was not the Apostle John.[32] It might seem curious that the words ''only Son'' show up only four times in the Bible, all by the same author. Such coincidences have led to a lot of study on the thoughts of John. Since the three letters of John were originally called the ''Johannine Letters'', such study has become called ''Johannine''.

An extensive study of Johannine thought is presented in The Anchor Bible[33] [hereafter called ''Anchor'']. This extensive Bible uses over 2000 pages to cover the gospel of John, a gospel which takes only 24 pages in the normal Bible. Therefore, Anchor uses almost 100 pages of text to describe and analyze each page of the gospel of John as found in the normal Bible. Obviously, Anchor is an extensive work; however, as mentioned by the General Editors, ''The Anchor Bible is aimed at the general reader with no special formal training in biblical studies; yet, it is written with the most exacting standards of scholarship, reflecting the highest

170

technical accomplishment.'' In other words, if anyone were to want to take the time and to make the effort, they could use Anchor in order to understand what Biblical scholars believe the Bible means when it uses certain words or phrases.

The following nine items are taken from Anchor. The first words in brackets show the reference page in Anchor, followed by the Biblical reference if needed. The part following the brackets is a direct copy from Anchor. The underlining is from Anchor. After these items are presented, then a short analysis or interpretation of these nine items will be made. Although each of these nine items has its own importance and merits understanding, the most important items for the major point being made in this section are items 7-9.

1. [Page CXXXVIII]   John 1: 1-18 is the Prologue. It is an early Christian hymn, probably stemming from Johannine circles, which has been adapted to serve as an overture to the Gospel narrative of the career of the incarnate Word.

2. [Page 11, John 1:12] John uses *tekna* for Children and uses *huios* only for Jesus. Yet, while John preserves a vocabulary difference between Jesus as God's son and Christians as God's children, it is in John that our present state as God's children on this earth comes out most clearly; I John 3:2 says, ''Beloved, we are God's children now; it does not yet appear what we shall be, but we know that when he appears we shall be like him, for we shall see him as he is.''

3. [Page 11, John 13]...in Johannine thought, those who believe and those begotten by God are equivalent: ''Everyone who believes that Jesus is the Messiah is begotten by God'' in I John 5:1.

4. [Page 12, John 13] John and I John never describe Jesus as having been begotten by God, but they do speak thus of those who follow Jesus.

5. [Page 12, John 13] Although the verb "begotten" can mean "born", in this case the idea of the agency [i.e. the seed that it comes from] is clearly more appropriate.

6. [Page 13, John 14] In reference to "And the Word became flesh", the word "flesh" refers to the whole man...and it is not said that the Word became a man but equivalently that the Word became man.

7. [Page 13, John 14] In reference to "as of the only Son", ...it may have been theologically desirable to avoid the reading "as of an only Son" lest someone interpret it to mean, "as if he were an only Son." The meaning of "as" is, of course, not "as if" but "in the quality of".

8. [Page 13, John 14] In reference to "only Son", the Greek term used is *monogenes* which literally means "of a single kind". Although *genos* is distantly related to *gennan* which means "to beget", there is little Greek justification for the translation of *monogenes* as "only begotten"...[but was a result] of the Vulgate on the King James Version of the Bible. Actually, John never uses the term "begotten" when referring to Jesus. *Monogenes* describes a quality of Jesus, his uniqueness, not what is called in Trinitarian theology his "procession." It reflects the Hebrew word *yahid* which means "only, precious" which is used in Genesis 22:2,12,16 of Abraham's son Isaac, as *monogenes* is used of Isaac in Hebrews 11:17. Isaac was Abraham's uniquely precious son, but not his only begotten son.

9. [Page 147, John 3:16] The theme of Jesus' death is introduced in John 3:14-5 and appears again in John 3:16. Just as that death was portrayed under the Old Testament symbol of the serpent in John 3:14-15, so there is seemingly an implicit reference to the Old Testament in the language of John 3:16. Abraham was

commanded to take his "only" son Isaac whom he <u>loved</u> to offer to the Lord [Genesis 22: 2,12]; many scholars [Wescott, Bernard, Barrett, Glasson] think that this lies behind John 3:16: "For God so loved the world that he gave his <u>only</u> Son, that whoever believes in him should not perish but have eternal life." Even the mention of "the world" fits in with this background, for Abraham's generosity in sacrificing his only son was to be beneficial to all the nations of the world [Genesis 22:18].

An analysis of these nine items would show that in item 1, Anchor is implying that the words of John 1-18 are meant as a hymn. By definition, a hymn is a song of praise or thanksgiving. Quite often, hymns of praise are intended to glorify and are not necessarily to be taken literally. In item 2, Anchor implies that because the Greek word used for Jesus is different than the Greek word used for us, then we are different. Items 3-5 imply that those who follow Jesus become as from the seed of God. Item 6 states that the Word became a part of mankind, not a man.

Item 7 becomes the first reference in the Bible to "only Son" and it says that in John 1:14 where "we have beheld his glory, glory as of the only Son from the Father" means that "we have beheld his glory, glory in the quality of the only Son from the Father".

Items 8 and 9 become the key, for in these two items which refer to John 1:18 and John 3:16, we find that the Greek word used in each is *monogenes* and that this is the same Greek word used to describe Isaac in Hebrews 11:17. We also know that Abraham had other sons. Genesis 25:2 lists six sons from his second wife, Keturah, after Sarah died. And in Gen. 21:9 is mentioned the son, Ishmael, whom Abraham had by Hagar, the Egyptian, even before Isaac's birth. Certainly Isaac was special to Abraham as indicated by the fact that Abraham gave all he had to him [Gen. 25:5]; but Isaac, special and precious as he was, was not Abraham's only son.

173

Hebrews 11:17-8 states, "By faith, Abraham, when he was tested, offered up Isaac, and he who had received the promises was ready to offer up his only son, of whom it was said, 'Through Isaac shall your descendents be named.'" Again, it has to be emphasized that in these verses, which harken back to Genesis 22:12, the word used for "only son" is the Greek word *monogenes* which is the same word used in referring to Jesus in John 1:18 and in John 3:16. In Gen.22:12, the word is the Hebrew word *yahid* which means "only" in the sense of being "special, precious". Again, special and precious as Isaac may have been to Abraham, he was not his only son. And the writer of John knew what he was doing when he used the same Greek word to define Jesus as a special, precious Son of God, but not necessarily the only one. However, just as Isaac may have been the only son of Abraham through whom God's plan for his people could be achieved, so might Jesus be the only son of God through whom His plan might be achieved. Neither would have to be the "only" [i.e. singular] son in order for this to be true.

Christians seem to have accepted Jesus as the only Son of God. They do it in the Apostle's Creed which was accepted by the Church about 1,200 years after the death of Jesus Christ, they do it by use of the English words "only Son" which appear four times in the Bible, and they do it by dogmas and scripture which teach that the Father and the Son are one. But the original language in which the scriptures were written does not say that Jesus Christ was the only son of God, just that he was a very precious and special son through whom His dreams would be realized, just as Isaac was to Abraham. The New Ager believes in the original description of Jesus as a precious and special son, but not the only one. And the New Ager also accepts that Jesus is one with God, just as we all can be if eternity lasts long enough.

2. CONCEIVED BY THE HOLY GHOST [OR BY THE POWER OF THE HOLY SPIRIT] Although there are some exceptions, most New Agers have absolutely no problem believing

that Jesus Christ was conceived by the Holy Ghost, although many would prefer the Catholic wording which says that he was conceived "by the power of the Holy Spirit". As described in Chapter 6, the New Ager believes that Spirit has tremendous power and can do essentially anything it wants to do if the entity will let it. Consequently, there is no problem accepting this belief about Jesus Christ, so long as the Apologetics don't try to change the Apostles' Creed by putting the word "only" in and stating that the Holy Spirit would not be able to do that for any other entity. Again, the New Ager believes that this happened for Jesus Christ; but the New Ager just does not accept that he was the only one for whom this has ever been done. The New Ager does not doubt Christ's divinity; merely that his divinity was exclusive for him alone. And the New Ager does not believe that Jesus ever stated that he was the only one who was divine. In fact, Jesus many times infers that where he goes, we can go also.

3. BORN OF THE VIRGIN MARY In relation to this part of the Apostles' Creed, there are two things that may surprise many Christians. The first is that there is probably a higher percentage of New Agers who believe in the virgin birth than there are Christians; and the second is that the virgin birth is not biblical. We will address the second issue first.

As mentioned in Chapter 3, only two of the four gospels mention the birth of Jesus. Those two gospels are Matthew and Luke. The reference in Luke will be discussed first.

In the story of the birth in Luke, the word "virgin" appears twice. Each time is in Luke 1:26-8 which states, "In the sixth month [of Elizabeth's pregnancy] the angel Gabriel was sent from God to a city of Galilee named Nazareth, to a virgin betrothed to a man whose name was Joseph, of the house of David; and the virgin's name was Mary." Notice that both times the word "virgin" was used, it was used when Mary was betrothed to Joseph--before they

175

were even married. Although those are the only times Luke uses the word "virgin", there is a fair amount of discussion in Luke 1:28-53 which implies that Mary conceived through the Holy Spirit and under the power of God. The implication, however, is not straightforward, and the "virgin birth" is not mentioned as such. As mentioned in the preceding section, the New Ager has absolutely no problem accepting the probability that the Holy Spirit was involved in the conception of Jesus. In fact, the New Ager believes that Spirit is involved in all activities into which we accept its involvement by our free-will choice.

In Matthew, the only reference to a virgin is the statement in Matt. 1:22-3 which states that the birth of Jesus "took place to fulfil what the Lord had spoken by the prophet: 'Behold, a virgin shall conceive and bear a son, and his name shall be called Emmanuel' [which means, God is with us]". Notice that Matthew is not stating that a virgin would give birth, but only that the birth fulfilled what the prophet had said. However, if one were to look at the reference cited for the prophet's statement, he would find it to be Isaiah 7:14 which states, "Therefore the Lord himself will give you a sign. Behold, a young woman shall conceive and bear a son and shall call his name Immanuel." Consequently, the term "virgin" used in Matthew refers to a physical age and not to a condition of sexual inexperience.

John Shelby Spong is the Episcopal bishop of Newark. In a recent book[34] he states, "When I became aware that neither the word virgin nor the concept of virginity appears in the Hebrew text of Isaiah that Matthew quoted to undergird his account of Jesus' virgin birth, I became newly aware of the fragile nature of biblical fundamentalism. The understanding of 'virgin' is present only in the Greek word *parthenos*, used to translate the Hebrew word *almah* in the Greek version of the Hebrew Scriptures. The Hebrew word for virgin is *betulah. Almah* never means 'virgin' in Hebrew. I had to face early on in my priestly career the startling possibility that the virgin tradition so deep in Christianity may well rest upon something as fragile as the weak reed of mistranslation.'' Later in the same book, he says, ''Matthew quoted a text from Isaiah to prove the virgin birth tradition. Fortunately for Matthew's integrity, he quoted that Hebrew text in Greek, where the connotation of 'virgin' is present in the Greek word *parthenos*. However, if he had gone to the original Hebrew, he would have discovered that the connotation of virginity was not present in the original text of Isaiah. The Hebrew word for 'virgin' was *betulah*. The word used in Isaiah is *almah*, which means 'young woman'. It does not mean virgin in any Hebrew text in the entire Bible in which it is used.''

And furthermore, as stated in Chapter 3, the words used in the Apostles' Creed are ''Virgin Mary'' capitalized more like a title than a description of sexual stature.

But despite all of that erudite discussion of the meaning of scripture, most New Agers believe that Jesus did have a virgin birth, and many believe that Mary did also. Thus, many New Agers will have beliefs similar to that of the Roman Catholic Church. However, these beliefs are not substantiated by the words of the Bible; they are substantiated by the words of Edgar Cayce. In Edgar Cayce's Story of Jesus[35] the following questions and answers appear:

Q. Is the teaching of the Roman Catholic Church correct, in that Mary was without original sin from the moment of her conception in the womb of Anne?

A. It would be correct in any case. Correct more in this. For as for the material teaching of that just referred to, you see, in the beginning, Mary was the twin soul of the Master in the entrance into the earth!

Q. Then neither Mary nor Jesus had a human father?

A. Neither Mary nor Jesus had a human father. They were one soul so far as the earth is concerned.

Because of this, many New Agers accept the virgin birth of Jesus, but not because of any inerrant words of scripture, for the scripture has been mistranslated in its conversion from the original languages in which it had been written. Instead, the New Ager accepts the virgin birth of Jesus because it readily can happen under power of Spirit and because it also happened in the case of Melchizedek [see Hebrews 7:3] who Edgar Cayce states was an earlier incarnation of the one who became the Christ. Because of this, three portions of scripture start to make sense to the New Ager. They are: [1] Genesis 14:18-20 in which Abraham meets Melchizedek and pays him homage; [2] John 8:56-8 in which Jewish leaders ask Jesus how he could have met Abraham when he [Jesus] is so young, and Jesus says, "Before Abraham was, I am."; and [3] Hebrews 7:2-3 in which Melchizedek is named as king of peace, "without father or mother or genealogy, and has neither beginning of days nor end of life, but resembling the Son of God he continues a priest forever." This description sounds a lot like a perfect description of Jesus Christ.

And so, the New Ager may accept the virgin birth of Jesus; but not as an event which has happened only once in the history of the world.

4. SUFFERED UNDER PONTIUS PILATE In nine out of the fourteen times in Mark that Jesus refers to himself as the "Son of man", he is referring to the suffering and death that he was going to be going through in being a servant to the people; for as it says in Mark 10:45, "For the Son of man also came not to be served but to serve, and to give his life as a ransom for many". It was a rather unusual situation for a God to suffer so that the people could be served. Prior to the appearance of Jesus Christ, most religions had proposed just the reverse: that the people would suffer so that the gods could be served. The New Ager believes that any experiences in which an entity makes another entity suffer is not an experience which is on the Way: it therefore may later become

an unresolved experience which must be resolved. Because of this belief, the New Ager has no problem with the belief that Jesus Christ suffered under Pontius Pilate. It is an experience of service which fits nicely into the overall belief system of the New Ager.

5. WAS CRUCIFIED, DEAD AND BURIED   As mentioned in Chapter 3, the crucifixion of the one called "King of the Jews" during the procuratorship of Pontius Pilate is a matter of public record in histories other than the Bible. It happened. Crucifixions happened thousands of times during the Roman occupation of Jerusalem and of other territories. It was the conventional method of execution. That it happened to Jesus Christ is not in dispute in any way.

6. HE ROSE AGAIN FROM THE DEAD This portion of the Apostles' Creed is imminently believed in by both the Christian and by the majority of the New Agers who feel that this is a very natural occurrence.

7. HE ASCENDED INTO HEAVEN It is quite possible that the ascension of Jesus Christ into heaven is more widely believed by the New Ager than it is by the Christian, for ascension is an Article of Faith in the New Age. Ascension is associated with multi-dimensional existences. There is no doubt in the mind of all New Agers that multi-dimensional entities are a common occurrence. Therefore it would be only natural to have an evolved Son of God such as Jesus Christ be multi-dimensional, *i.e.* capable of ascension at any time. Other such entities in the Bible who have ascended are Enoch [Genesis 5:24] and Melchizedek [Hebrews 7:3]. According to Edgar Cayce, both of these incarnates had previously held the soul of the entity who later incarnated as Jesus Christ. Again as in the case of all six attributes previously discussed, the New Ager does not doubt this characteristic of Christ. The New Ager believes that he ascended into heaven because he is divine; but again, that his divinity is not an exclusive thing.

179

8. HE SHALL COME TO JUDGE THE LIVING AND THE DEAD The New Ager feels that nothing expresses his belief quite as well as this does. Jesus Christ is of the Spirit. That is one of the definitions of the Trinity as espoused by Christian dogma. Since he is of the Spirit and the Spirit is also of God, then he becomes a part of the hierarchy in which helpful judgments go on all the time. These would include such judgments as to whether or not this live entity [i.e. presently incarnate] is handling or is not handling his present experiences; or as to whether or not this entity whose Soul is back with us [i.e. not presently incarnate] did or did not handle his experiences; or as to what, Soul willing, his next set of experiences will entail. Such an evaluative interchange is one of the keystones of the New Age system of beliefs. Consequently, the New Ager has absolutely no problem with this characteristic of Jesus Christ.

In SUMMARY, the New Ager could recite the portion of the Apostles' Creed which refers to Jesus Christ about as well as most Christians could. The only exception that he would have would be with the word ''only'' in reference to any of the characteristics presented; for again, the New Ager has no question about the divinity of Christ--only his exclusivity. And although the typical Christian might not want to accept it, the exclusivity of Jesus Christ is not biblical. Instead, it is a concept which has been developed by man during his debates to generate doctrines and dogmas which the faithful could understand and by which they would be identified. It is a direct result of accepting, and possibly mishandling, the Great Commission given to man by Christ.

HOLY SPIRIT

The Apologetics state that ''throughout the Bible the Holy Spirit is depicted as a distinct, divine Person. In Acts 13:2,4 we see the Holy Spirit referred to as a Person and even directly quoted,

180

something that can only be done of a person. Several verses in the Bible assert the deity of the Holy Spirit. Words attributed to Jehovah in the Old Testament are in Hebrews 3:7-11 attributed to the Holy Spirit. The Holy Spirit has always been truly God, and He exists eternally [Hebrews 9:14]"[36] This quotation is presented in a section of the book which is intended to show how the "I AM" Ascended Masters' movement was not Christian because, among other reasons, they did not believe in the Person of the Holy Spirit.

Other scripture quoted by the Apologetics to defend the "person" of the Holy Spirit include Acts 13:2 which says, "While they were worshiping the Lord and fasting, the Holy Spirit said, 'Set apart for me Barnabas and Saul for the work to which I have called them.' ''; and Acts 13:4 which says, "So, being sent out by the Holy Spirit, they went down to Seleucia; and from there they sailed to Cyprus."; and Hebrews 9:14 which says, "how much more shall the blood of Christ, who through the eternal Spirit offered himself without a blemish to God, purify your conscience from dead works to serve the living God."; and finally Hebrews 3:7-11 in which the Holy Spirit gives an Old Testament quotation.

There are two important points to be made about the scriptures chosen by the Apologetics to prove their point. The first is that the word "Person" is not used in any of them to describe the Holy Spirit; and the second is that these scriptures are wholly supportive of the New Age concept of Spirit.

In respect to the word "Person" and its concept, this gets into the whole issue of the three "Persons of the Trinity" which will be addressed in the next section. In respect to the New Age concept of Spirit, the New Ager believes that all Spirit is of God, is sent by God and speaks for God as it works with Soul to guide the experiential journey of the entity. What better support of this concept could there be than that which is presented in Hebrews 9:14?

With the exception of the concept of ''Person'' which is addressed in the next section, the New Ager sees no conflict with the Apologetics' definition of the Holy Spirit, for what good is a helper sent from God if one can't talk with him?

THE TRINITY

One of the major cases made by the Apologetics in defense of Christianity and against the New Age movement is that the New Ager does not accept the Christian dogma of the Trinity as represented by the three Persons of the Father, the Son and the Holy Ghost [or Spirit]. They are probably right.

The word ''Trinity'' does not appear in the Bible; and neither does the word ''Person'' or ''Persons'' as used in the definition of the Trinity. The concept of the Trinity was developed over a number of years through much debate and with the help of a considerable amount of speculative theology. The historical development of the Trinity is presented in The Encyclopaedia Britannica, Vol. 16, pages 351-2. The following several paragraphs represent a summary of that presentation.

The Christian doctrine of the Trinity had its foundation in the earliest Christian experiences and is based on the fact that God came to meet Christians in a threefold figure: [1] as the Old Testament Creator, Father and Judge who was the Lord of history; [2] as Jesus Christ who lived among them and showed himself as being resurrected; and [3] as the Holy Spirit whom they experienced as the power of the new life and the potency of the Kingdom of God. The real question then became how to reconcile this encounter with three Gods with their faith in the oneness of God, for the oneness of God was a major tenet which distinguished the Jew and the Christian from the pagans. This became a real puzzle which generated many possible solutions.

The first puzzle which had to be resolved concerned the figure of Jesus Christ. The gospel of John presented the eternal divinity of Jesus; whereas the gospel of Mark presented the Baptism of Jesus Christ as the adoption of the man Jesus Christ into the Sonship of God through the descent of the Holy Spirit. This situation became worse, because whereas in the early days Jesus Christ was known as an historical figure, the Holy Spirit was viewed not as a personal figure but rather as a power which appeared graphically only in the form of a dove.

The first attempt to solve this problem of the ''figure'' of Christ and the ''non-figure'' of the Holy Spirit came from Johannine thinking influenced by Neoplatonic Logos philosophy. As previously mentioned ''Johannine'' refers to the work of John. Neoplatonism is the philosophy introduced by Plotinus in the 3rd century AD. It survived through the 6th century and represented the final form of pagan Greek philosophy. Within this philosophy, Logos refers to cosmic reason or order. In Neoplatonic philosophy, God was seen as a transcendent God, *i.e.* He is pre-eminent and He is outside of all things. He then sends a part of himself [the Son] forth to do His work, but by so doing, the part that goes forth becomes diminished in power because of its distance from the transcendent origin and of its approach to or incorporation into physical things. In other words, in this philosophy, when a God incarnates, his power is diminished. In this manner, if Neoplatonic philosophy were to be carried to its extreme, then the three ways in which God met the Christian would evolve into Gods of unequal power which would therefore be a polytheistic hierarchy.

The Christian community insisted on the complete sameness of essence of the three manifestations. In addition, they proposed that Christian Logos [i.e. cosmic reason or order] meant Christ as the second part of this three-way manifestation. However another problem soon surfaced, for if there were a triplicity of equally ranked gods, this would displace the idea of the oneness of God.

By the third century, the debate waxed enthusiastically, particularly as represented by the Arian controversy. Arius believed so strongly in the concept of the oneness of God that he had to dispute the oneness of essence of the Son and the Holy Spirit with God the Father. Such debates led to concepts which had absolutely no biblical foundation, such as the ''sameness of Essence or *homoousia*'' vs. the ''similarity of essence or *homoiousia*'' of divine beings. In other words, the debate went so far as to wonder whether divine beings were the same, or merely similar. As a part of this debate, Arius became a believer in angel-Christology which proposed that the Son of God was the highest of God's angels and was sent to Earth to become Jesus Christ. In this way, the Son was not God and the oneness of God could be preserved. However, it was argued that if the Son were not God, then how could he redeem the world? With the belief that such an approach to solving the puzzle would toss out redemption and salvation, the Arian controversy ended.

Later, Augustine tried to resolve the puzzle by coupling the threeness of God with the threeness of man [mind, body and soul] as postulated by Plato. His justification was that man was made in the image of God. Another proposal was that of Joachim of Fiore who proposed three consecutive periods of salvation of the world: one by the Father, the second by the Son and the third by the Holy Spirit. This was considered to be heresy from the outset.

The final dogmatic formulation of the Trinitarian doctrine was presented in the Athanasian Creed of the early sixth century. It went back to the formulation of Tertullian. Tertullian was a Christian theologian who lived in Carthage in the second century. He instituted many concepts. As one example, he became the major proponent of using ecclesiastical Latin as the accepted language of the Western Church. He also proposed a method of how three Gods could exist in one person. By initiating ecclesiastical Latin, he influenced western Christianity for almost 1600 years. By formulating a definition of the Trinity, he influenced Christianity for all time. He later left the Christian church because he felt that it was becoming too associated with the world. He become a Montanist. The formulation for the Trinity proposed by Tertullian and accepted some three hundred years later after much debate was *una substantia--tres personae*, or "one substance--three persons". In practical terms it was no solution to the puzzle whatsoever, for it resolved nothing. It was merely a compromise which held fast to both basic ideas of the Christian revelation--to the oneness of God and to his self-revelation in the figures of the Father, the Son, and the Holy Spirit--without rationalizing the mystery of how this could be at all. And furthermore, this compromise does not address the question posed by Mark 13:32 which says, "But of that day or that hour no one knows, not even the angels in heaven nor the Son, but only the Father." Surely if one part of the Trinity knows something which the other parts do not know, it stands to reason that they can not be totally equal.

There are many other examples which substantiate the belief that trinitarian concepts create almost as many questions as answers. In fact, throughout the history of Christianity, the concept of the Trinity has been debated and questioned by almost all of the world's great thinkers, philosophers, and theologians. Today, the mystery of the Trinity continues to confound. Those who question it say that it is not biblical, that it floated around for over three hundred years before it was accepted as doctrine, and that it answers all questions about it with a non-answer. As Bishop Spong, an Episcopal bishop has written, "I am not interested in preserving the doctrine of the Trinity. I do not believe that the ultimate truth of God has been captured in the trinitarian formula. I am passionately interested in understanding why the doctrine of the Trinity was a life-and-death issue during the early centuries of

Christian history. I am eager to embrace the experience out of which the doctrine of Trinity was forged and the truth to which this doctrine points. There is, however, nothing sacred or eternal for me about the words previous generations chose to be the bearers of their truth.''[37] Bishop Spong is saying that absolute belief in the Trinity is not as important as understanding why the concept that there be a Trinity was so important to the early Christians; for in this way, we can help to understand what elements from Christianity are important for us to debate today.

Apologetics like to make an ''acid test'' to determine if someone is a Christian. They seem to want to make an ''acid test'' out of the definition of God and out of the definition of the Trinity. Neither can be defined. Each is ineffable. It is the belief of the New Ager that one can believe in God, in Jesus Christ, in the Holy Spirit and in all the others who work for/with Them without resorting to a Trinitarian formulation which answers no questions.

MANKIND

Apologetics propose that man can never be God for man is the created whereas God is the Creator. By this differentiation, God becomes infinite and man finite. They also declare that man is not good, but he is sinful and can not be reconciled to God except through the sacrifice of Jesus Christ. They go on to use four biblical references to substantiate this point. The references they chose are: Ezekiel 28:2-9; Isaiah 47:8-11; Romans 3:23; and I John 1:18.[38]

As a short summary of these references, Ezekiel says that man is a man and not a god, and since he calls himself a god, then the real God will bring all sorts of calamities down upon him and he will die. None of this would happen if he really were a god. Isaiah says essentially the same thing. Romans says, ''since all have sinned and fall short of the glory of God''. I John tells us that the antichrist is coming.

The New Ager does not believe he is perfect, for if he were, he wouldn't be having an experiential existence solely in this physical plane. Instead, he would have ascended and be helping others through a multi-dimensional series of experiences. Therefore, no entity who has not achieved multi-dimensional status can be considered anything other than a normal man with all of the limited capabilities but unlimited potential of a normal man. While in this state, he certainly falls short of the glory of God. However, by working with Spirit, he feels that at some time within the time limits of eternity, he can become multi-dimensional and therefore be where God was. He believes this for many reasons, some of which are biblical. As a few examples to support this belief:

1. Man is created in the image of God [Genesis 1:27 and other places];
2. Every one who believes that Jesus is the Christ is a child of God [I John 5:1];
3. Every one who follows Jesus is begotten of God [i.e. from the seed of God]. This reasoning is presented in the Anchor references 4 and 5 in the preceding section entitled ''Jesus Christ'';
4. For all who are led by the Spirit of God are sons of God [Romans 8:14]; and
5. On and on it could go.

It is a fact of physical life on this physical plane that given time, it is possible that the son or the daughter of a father can do everything that the father can do. Thus the child, given time, can develop all the capabilities of the parent. The New Ager feels that this possibility applies to his relationship with God also, even though it may take an eternity of being led by Spirit before it would show.

There is one more point which should be made here. The Apologetics make a big point about the fact [their word] that whereas Jesus is the real Son of God, we can only become adopted sons; and therefore we can never be anything like either Jesus or God no matter how long eternity is. They quote five verses of scripture to substantiate this point.[39] Those five verses of scripture are from the King James Version [KJV] of the Bible which does use the word "adoption" the following five times: Romans 8:15; 8:23; 9:4; Gal. 4:5; and Eph. 1:5. The Revised Standard Version [RSV] uses the word only two times. In Romans 8:15, the KJV says "Spirit of adoption", whereas the RSV says "spirit of sonship". In Romans 9:4, the KJV says "Who are Israelites to whom pertaineth the adoption...of God"; whereas the RSV says "They are the Israelites, and to them belong the sonship...God who is over all be blessed for ever." In Ephesians 1:5, the KJV says " Having predestinated us unto the adoption of children by Jesus Christ to himself"; whereas the RSV says, "He destined us in love to be his sons through Jesus Christ".

The definition of "sonship" is "the fact or relationship of being a son". Consequently, based on what is widely accepted to be the standard version of the Bible for English-speaking countries, there are only two references which use the word "adoption" in any way. Those two times are in Romans 8:23, which says, "but we ourselves, who have the first fruits of the Spirit, groan inwardly as we wait for adoption as sons, the redemption of our bodies"; and in Galatians 4:5 which says, "God sent forth his Son, born of woman, born under the law, to redeem those who were under the law, so that we might receive adoption as sons". Galatians then goes on in verses 6-7 to say, "And because you are sons, God has sent the Spirit of his Son into our hearts, crying 'Abba! Father!' So through God you are no longer a slave but a son, and if a son then an heir." In other words, the final reference in the RSV of the Bible which use the word "adoption" is followed by strong statements that we are to be God's sons and heirs.

188

But the real question to ask is whether or not there is any qualitative difference between an adopted son and a natural son. Although in modern society some people may feel that an adopted child is not equal in all respects to a natural child, the Bible was not written in modern times. The key to this entire debate is the fact that all references to adoption were written by Paul, and that is true whether considering the five references in the KJV or the two references in the RSV. Consequently it is important to know what Paul thought about the qualitative aspects of adoption.

Paul was a Jew, but he was also a highly educated Roman citizen. Because of his education and family status, Paul would have been very aware of Roman law. Because of his training as a Pharisee, he would also have been very aware of Hebrew law; but the writing in which the word ''adoption'' appears is in Paul's letters addressed to churches in Rome, in Ephesus and in Galatia, all of which were under Roman, not Hebrew law. Consequently, when trying to inform people about God's relationship with mankind, he would use concepts with which they were familiar-- with the concepts of Roman law.

In a definitive commentary, William Barclay, the great Scottish New Testament interpreter, spends several pages on the meaning of ''adoption''.[40] They are summarized in the following paragraphs.

''Paul is introducing us to another of the great metaphors in which he describes the new relationship of the Christian to God. He speaks of the Christian being adopted into the family of God. It is only when we understand how serious and complicated a step Roman adoption was that we really understand the depth of meaning in this passage.

Roman adoption was always rendered more serious and more difficult by the Roman *patria protestas*. This was the father's power over his family; it was the power of absolute disposal and control, and in the early days was actually the power of life and death. In regard to his father, the Roman son never came of age. No matter how old he was, he still came under the *patria protestas*, in the absolute possession and under the absolute control of his father. Obviously, this made adoption into another family a very difficult and serious step. In adoption a person had to pass from one *patria protestas* to another.

There were two steps. The first was known as *manipatio* [during which a son was symbolically sold and repurchased two times and on the third sale, he was let go]. There followed a ceremony called *vindicatio* [during which the adopting father presented the legal reasons for adoption to the Roman authorities] to transfer the person to be adopted into his *patria protestas*. [These four ceremonies] complete the adoption. Clearly this was a serious and impressive step.

But it is the consequences of adoption which are most significant for the picture that is in Paul's mind. There are four main ones: [1] the adopted person lost all rights in his old family and gained all the rights of a legitimate son in his new family. In the most binding legal way, he got a new father; [2] it followed that he became heir to his new father's estate. Even if other sons were afterwards born, it did not effect his rights. He was inalienably co-heir with them; [3] in law, the old life of the adopted person was completely wiped out; for instance, all debts were cancelled. He was regarded as a new person entering into a new life with which the past had nothing to do; [4] in the eyes of the law he was absolutely the son of his new father.

Roman history provides an outstanding case of how completely this was held to be true. The Emperor Claudius adopted Nero in order that he might succeed him on the throne; they were not in any sense blood relatives. Claudius already had a daughter, Octavia. To cement the alliance, Nero wished to marry her. Nero and Octavia were in no sense blood relations; yet, in the eyes of the law, they were brother and sister; and before they could marry, the

Roman senate had to pass special legislation.

That is what Paul is thinking of. He uses still another picture from Roman adoption. He says that God's spirit witnesses with our spirit that we really are his children. The adoption ceremonies were carried out in the presence of seven witnesses [so that a witness could step forth in the case of any dispute] and swear that the adoption was genuine....So it is the Holy Spirit himself who is the witness to our adoption into the family of God.

We see then that every step of Roman adoption was meaningful in the mind of Paul when he transferred the picture to our adoption into the family of God....The old life has no more rights over us; God has absolute right...we begin a new life with God and become heirs of all his riches...joint-heirs with Jesus Christ...what he inherits, we also inherit [including suffering and] we also inherit [Christ's] life and glory.''

This is powerful commentary on Paul's thoughts when he writes to people under Roman law that they are to be adopted into God's family. It states that in all senses, when adopted into God's family they [and we] are to be considered equal in a qualitative sense to Jesus Christ as a son of God. Roman adoption differs from our present concept of adoption in several meaningful ways.

But all of this discussion about the differences between the Apologist and the New Ager in respect to mankind boils down to one major difference in belief: the Apologists believe that man is not god and never can be; whereas the New Ager believes that man is not god, but through continuing guidance by Spirit can be where God was even though getting there may take an eternity.

SALVATION

In a very general sense, the primary purpose of any religion is to provide salvation for its adherents, with salvation meaning the deliverance from conditions such as suffering, evil, finitude [i.e. the quality of being finite] or death.

The Apologetics believe that salvation comes not from works, but by God's Grace freely given through Jesus Christ, and only through Jesus Christ.

There are many in the New Age movement who do not believe that the need for salvation is such a big deal, for it is merely another experience along the Way and therefore any need for deliverance from anything is merely the handling of another unresolved issue which has to be resolved before progress can be continued. However, they also believe that such "Karmic issues" can be forgiven. They merely believe that whereas Jesus Christ is one forgiver, he is not the only one.

Other New Agers accept the concept of salvation as being a fairly big deal in that it is associated with the concept of Grace. In fact, many New Agers feel that their belief in Grace exceeds that of the typical Christian, with Grace being defined as "the divine love and protection given by a loving God whether merited by the receiver or not."

Many religions establish methods or techniques for receiving grace. One of these is the use of rituals. Those which apply to the Christian and the New Ager are presented in Chapter 4. Other methods such as the generation of knowledge or the dedication of devotion and service are also accepted by many religions.

But few religions accept salvation as the primary purpose of the religion to the extent that Christianity does. The Christian believes that: [1] man deserves to be damned by God for the original sin which he inherits from Adam as well as for his own sins; [2] Christ saved man from eternal damnation and from his own sins by the crucifixion which was a sacrifice paid for all mankind; and [3] belief in the saving power of Jesus Christ is basic to the religion and finds expression in every aspect of its faith and practice.

The New Ager would counter by stating that a loving God would never place one of His Children into the condition of eternal damnation by any activity presented by that child during his eighty years on this Earth, whether that activity was one of commission or of omission. The New Ager believes that in respect to eternity, eighty years or so is as one grain of sand within the Sahara Desert; and in respect to the universe, Earth is likewise as a grain of sand within a vast desert. To expect a loving God to permit only this limited amount of time and space before rejecting us would be as if a devoted father were to say to his twelve month old son, "If you are not potty-trained within the next five minutes, then I will never hug you." No loving father would do that; and Jesus never stated that his Father had put any time limitations onto His people or else they would face eternal damnation. In fact, neither Jesus nor any of the Apostles present the words "eternal damnation" in the scriptures. The closest is "eternal sin" [Mark 3:29] or "eternal punishment" [Matt. 25:46], each used only once. In contrast, the scriptures use the term "eternal life" twenty-nine [29] different times! In general, the New Ager rejects the concept of eternal damnation and accepts, instead, the belief that before the end of eternity, all will spend an eternal life in the presence of God.

In summation, although the typical New Ager feels strongly about Grace, he will have a difficult time making a big issue about salvation, for he will feel that it is just "the way the cards are dealt" and that it is to be dealt with through participation in the experiential system of beliefs. In addition, the New Ager never seems to feel the lack of freedom which Christians seem to feel until they receive salvation. It is probable that this lack of freedom is based on fear which the acceptance of the concept of original sin and other sins have placed on the Christian. Fear is a powerful force in creating control and a subsequent sense of not being free. It is a force which will always be present when Ego rather than Spirit leads. It is a force which is rarely sensed or found in those New Agers who participate in their religion outside of the Ego-directed sects or cults.

MISCELLANEOUS BELIEFS

There are certain other beliefs of the New Age movement with which the Apologetics would take exception. They are presented in this separate section because they did not conveniently fit into the outline used by the Apologetics. Among others, they include Missions of Jesus the Christ; Order of Melchizedek; and Office of the Christ.

MISSIONS OF JESUS THE CHRIST refers to two beliefs on the part of the New Ager about the purpose of Christ's mission which are not expressed within orthodox Christianity. The first of these is expressed in the Bible, but not interpreted as the New Ager would believe. The second in merely inferred in the Bible.

The first concerns the brotherhood of man. Jesus called himself the ''Son of man'' more often than he used any other title. Drane presents several pages trying to express all the meanings and interpretations which have been placed on this title and calls it ''one of the most hotly disputed subjects in modern study of the New Testament.''[41] In addition, Jesus said, ''I and the Father are one.'' [John 10:30] The New Ager believes that in calling himself the Son of man, Jesus was telling us that he is just like us and that since he is one with the Father, than so are we. In this sense, the brotherhood of man has been established which is qualitatively one with God. This fits with the ''image of God'' part of the Creation story, and makes understandable the sayings of Jesus when he says that ''no one knows who the Son is except the Father, or who the Father is except the Son and any one to whom the Son chooses to reveal him.'' [Luke 10:22] Since the word ''him'' in this reference is not capitalized, then Jesus was not referring to the Father, but

194

instead to himself; and since Jesus reveals himself to us as being the Son of man [i.e. just like us], he has therefore revealed to us the Father who is "one with him/us". In no way does this mean that we are gods; only that given enough time and Spirit-led experiences, we can be where God was because we are like Him, qualitatively [*i.e.* in kind] but not quantitatively [*i.e.* in scope] for God is All. As some have expressed, each drop of water in the ocean is qualitatively but not quantitatively like the ocean itself; for the ocean is all, whereas each drop is only a similar part of the all. The New Ager believes that the passing on of this message is one purpose of Jesus' mission, and that there is substantial biblical justification for that belief.

A second mission purpose has only a minor amount of biblical justification. That is the belief on the part of the New Ager that Jesus elevated womanhood back to where she belonged and out of the lower status into which she had been placed for centuries by the male. There are biblical scenes which could be used to justify this belief such as the woman at the well and the adoration which Jesus seemed to put on both of the Marys [i.e. Mother Mary and Mary Magdalene]; but the major justification in this belief is that which comes from Channelers and other such interpreters of the things outside of the understanding of our physical senses. It is the New Agers belief that the status of the woman has not made as much progress as it should have in the 2,000 years since Jesus emphasized it; but that is the fault of Ego-driven rather than Spirit-driven desires. It is the belief of the New Ager that woman is a representative of God equal in all respects to the other part of the duality. It is also the belief of the New Ager that duality will be replaced by oneness within the time limits of eternity. It is the belief of the New Ager that one of the major parts of Jesus' mission to Earth was to institute such a direction.

ORDER OF MELCHIZEDEK The New Ager believes

that the Order of Melchizedek is a brotherhood encompassing mankind and multi-dimensional ones which has an extremely important role to play in bringing God together with His physical creatures. To understand this role requires some understanding of the person of Melchizedek.

Melchizedek is one of the mystery figures of the Bible. There are eleven references to Melchizedek in the Bible; one in Genesis [14:18]; one in Psalms [110:4]; and nine in Hebrews, most of which are similar to 5:6 [Thou art a priest forever after the order of Melchizedek] in which the ''Thou'' refers to Jesus Christ.

In Genesis, Melchizedek is called, ''king of Salem...and priest of God Most High''. Abraham blessed him and paid tithe to him. In other words, Abraham, the Father of our Judeo-Christian heritage paid homage to Melchizedek even before he started to fulfill his covenant with God. In this reference, the name Melchizedek means ''King of Rightousness'' and the name Salem means ''Peace''. Therefore, Melchizedek is the first King of Peace and Rightousness mentioned in the Bible. He is, in essence, an entity who foretold the coming of the Christ to Earth.

In Psalms, we have God mentioning for the first time the order of Melchizedek. In addition, in this Psalm, attributed to David, we have the fact that God could make an entity a ''priest for ever after the order of Melchizedek'' mentioned as one of the three great things that God can do.

The most important message from the nine references about Melchizedek in the book of Hebrews is that Jesus Christ was made a priest forever after the order of Melchizedek.

But who or what was Melchizedek and why was Jesus named by God to be a priest forever after the order of Melchizedek? The book of Hebrews goes to great length to answer this question.

196

First, Hebrews explains why it was important for Jesus to become a priest forever after the order of Melchizedek. Next, Hebrews explains why that makes Jesus a greater priest than any other priest whom the Jews could possibly follow. Finally, Hebrews presents the thought that Christianity is a greater and more perfect religion than Judaism could ever become. The argument is:

1. Melchizedek is greater than Abraham for three reasons. The first has to do with the kingship of Melchizedek. The name Melchizedek comes from the Hebrew words ''melek'' which means ''king'', and ''sedeq'' which means ''righteousness''. Also, he is king of Salem, which means ''peace''. Thus his kingship is that of righteousness and peace, and he is the first in the Bible to be so designated. The second has to do with the priesthood of Melchizedek. He is not simply named as being ''a priest'' but instead is designated as ''priest of God Most High'', and he is the first in the Bible to be so designated. The third has to do with tithing. Abram gave Melchizedek a tenth of everything that he had. Later, the Levite priests were tithed, but only by the descendents of Abraham. Since Abraham himself paid a tithe to Melchizedek, then Melchizedek not only is greater than Abraham, he is greater than the Levite priests all of whom are descendents of Abraham;

2. Melchizedek is a symbol of timeless priesthood. The Old Testament usually identifies each of its great men by not only noting his birth and death, but also by naming his parents and children. But Melchizedek appears on the scene with no introduction and equally disappears without note. He stands therefore as a timeless figure of priesthood and is in that sense, a priest for all time or a priest forever. This differs from the Levitical priests who are priests only for their earthly existence; and

3. Therefore, if Jesus were named by God to be ''a priest for ever after the order of Melchizedek'', then Jesus is not only greater than the angels, and greater than Moses, he is a greater

priest than any whom the Jews could follow. And the author of Hebrews goes on in Chapter 8 to admonish the Jews to follow the priest who sits on the right hand of God in Heaven, and not to follow the priests whom they can see on Earth.

For Christians, the discussion in Hebrews flows a little differently. In essence:

1. If Christ were to be a priest forever, then he would be eternally available to intercede on the behalf of his followers. In order to do this, God named His Son as a priest for ever after the order of Melchizedek, or as a priest for ever in the manner of Melchizedek, or as a priest for ever as a successor to Melchizedek, all of which have been presented in various translations of the Bible. In whatever manner Christ became a priest forever, God thus gave His followers their direct pipeline to Him, not through earthly priests, but by allowing them to come to the Father through the eternal priesthood of Jesus Christ; and

2. Although New Testament writers would often relate a present-day personage to one of the ''men of Old'' such as Moses or the like, the writer of Hebrews does not do this for the Christians. Instead of having the Son of God resemble Melchizedek, the writer has Melchizedek resembling the Son of God [Hebrews 7:3]. In this manner, he lets Christians know that Christ was in existence even before Melchizedek made his appearance, and that Christ was and is eternally available.

In the 1930s and 40s, Dr. Charles R. Erdman wrote commentaries on all the books of the New Testament. These commentaries continue to hold their place today as a standard reference work for Bible students. In his commentary on Hebrews, Dr. Erdman says:

''The majestic figure of Melchizedek stands for one short

198

scene upon the stage of history and then disappears forever into the mystery from which it emerged. However, an unfading halo of glory surrounds his very name, for this royal priest is an accepted type of Christ. His story is regarded as foreshadowing the essential feature in the priesthood of our Lord, namely its abiding efficacy. Indeed, it is interpreted as attesting the finality of the Christian faith.''

Then after several paragraphs of history and story which we have already covered, Dr. Erdman concludes with this paragraph:

''Here, also, is an implied message for the followers of Christ: If His abiding and unchanging priesthood is typified by the priesthood of Melchizedek, then He may be expected to bless all those who, like Abraham, are true servants of God; and all who receive blessings from Him should render Him honor and homage, even as Abraham offered to Melchizedek tithes of the chief spoils of war''.

Based on the book of Hebrews, a few insights into the Order of Melchizedek would suggest:

1. ''For ever'' is certainly different than ''for a lifetime''; and although all priests are to be respected, a priest would be able to act differently if he were to become a priest for ever. Having Christ as a priest for ever in the Order of Melchizedek has certainly meant a great deal to Christians, for he is eternally available to intercede on their behalf;

2. Melchizedek was a priest of God Most High before God started to work through Abraham. In other words, Melchizedek pre-dated Abraham, but since he resembled Christ, then Christians could logically take their Judeo-Christian heritage back to a time before Abraham;

3. Since Melchizedek is a priest for ever, and since Christ resembles Melchizedek, then there is evidence for the eternality of Christ to add to that presented in the early part of John's Gospel; and

4. Jesus was not a Levite. Instead, he was of the tribe of Judah. Therefore, despite what the Jews may have thought of him as a teacher, Jesus was not a priest to them. He was not of the priestly tribe. However, for Jesus to be named a ''priest for ever, after the order of Melchizedek'' means that he was made a priest in an order that was established before there were tribes. This means that not only could Jesus become a priest, so can anyone, whatever the tribal origin of his birth.

Because of its importance to the understanding of how Christ can intercede forever, the Order of Melchizedek becomes very important to the Christian. It also is of vital importance to the New Ager, many of whom consider themselves to be priests or priestesses in the Order of Melchizedek, and many of whom consider themselves to be workers in bringing God together with His physical creatures.

OFFICE OF THE CHRIST   The book of Hebrews begins with two verses which read ''In many and various ways God spoke of old to our fathers by the prophets; but in these last days he has spoken to us by the Son, whom he appointed the heir of all things, through whom he also created the world.'' The text then goes on to say that the Son is superior to the angels and that no angel has been called son by God.

The Anchor Bible[42] calls these verses ''God's latest word'' and makes two pertinent comments about them. The first comment refers to ''Son, whom he has appointed heir of all things''. As Paul says in Galatians 4:1, ''I mean that the heir, as long as he is a child,

200

is no better than a slave, though he is the owner of all the estate; but he is under guardians and trustees until the date set by the father.'' Thus, by appointing the Son heir, God has ''set the date'' and has replaced the previous guardians and trustees to whom he had previously entrusted the world by appointing the Son as his heir. The second comment refers to ''through whom he also created the world''. The Anchor Bible suggests that the best connotational translation of the Greek word *aionas* is probably ''ages'' thus giving, ''through whom he also created the ages''.

In a later part of the book of Hebrews there are three verses [2:9-11] which say, ''But we see Jesus, who for a little while was made lower than the angels, crowned with glory and honor because of the suffering of death, so that by the grace of God he might taste death for every one. For it was fitting that he, for whom and by whom all things exist, in bringing many sons to glory, should make the pioneer of their salvation perfect through suffering. For he who sanctifies and those who are sanctified have all one origin. That is why he is not ashamed to call them brethren''.

The entire sequence of Hebrews from its beginning through 2:9, is to make the point that although for a short time Jesus was made lower than the angels, he has been made greater than the angels by the fact of having been appointed the ''heir to all things''. The purpose of 2:10-11 is to say that all who are sanctified by the sanctifier come from the same origin, namely from God; and all who come from God are brothers, especially fully accepted brothers to Jesus Christ.

In the period during which Hebrews and Galatians were written, the son who became the ''heir to all things'' became the inheritor not only of the estate, but also of the staff who had previously managed the estate for the father. In other words, the ''guardians and trustees'' mentioned in Galatians who previously had held ''all things'' in trust for the son until the father ''set the date" as mentioned in Hebrews, now function for the son just as they had for the son's father; and in so doing, they participate in a brotherhood composed of "the sanctified ones" who are brothers.

As previously stated in Chapter 5, the New Ager believes that ascension is an occurrence which has happened more than just the once that it is mentioned in the Apostles' Creed. In fact, the New Ager believes that there are many who have ascended and work within multi-dimensional experiences to aid mankind whether in this particular physical plane or in another. Some of those ascended ones were the guardians and trustees used by God prior to having "set the date" at which the Son became the inheritor of "all things". They constitute the "Office of the Christ" which is defined as "The Redemptive Office of Divine Light encompassing the work of the 144,000 Ascended Masters working with YHWH and Michael through Jesus the Christ for the purification of this fallen universe. This includes all of the Ascended Masters who work for the liberation of man throughout the world in all eons of time". This is done through Jesus the Christ "through whom he [God] also made the ages".[43]

In the Office of the Christ are many who work through Jesus the Christ to fulfill God's purpose. The New Ager believes that it was this Office that Christ was referring to when he said "no one comes to the Father but by me" [John 14:6], for the entire Office works with YHWH through Jesus the Christ. Therefore, no effort of any Ascended Master reaches YHWH except through Jesus the Christ.

SUMMARY

This Chapter has presented a discussion of the New Age religion as contrasted to the Christian religion presented by the Apologetics. The discussion was necessary because the mature New Ager believes that his religion is very close to Christianity as practiced by the early Christians of about 2,000 years ago. To defend that position and to tie in with the Articles of Faith for the New Ager [see Chapter 6] as contrasted to the Articles of Faith for the Christian as represented by the Apostles' Creed has taken a fairly extensive amount of discussion. This section of this Chapter will attempt to overview that discussion.

The Apologetics believe that every one in the New Age movement belongs to a CULT. The New Ager disagrees. One Article of Faith for the New Ager is belief in what has become called "reincarnation". As mentioned in this Chapter, a fairly definitive study has proposed that some 65 million people in the U.S. believe in reincarnation. If true, then there are almost as many people who believe in reincarnation as belong to Protestant churches! In no way is membership in "cults" this large. The majority of New Agers do not belong to cults. Instead, they meet, study and worship in private homes or in small centers.

The Apologetics believe that the New Age follows SPIR-ITS which are false as defined by I John 4:1-3. However, because the mature New Ager believes in the Office of the Christ, then all which comes to him comes through Jesus the Christ whose birth name means "God is with us". The New Ager, therefore, believes that Jesus came in the flesh. This belief fulfills the requirements of the test presented in I John.

The Apologetics believe that the New Age religion is EASTERN. As Articles of Faith, the New Ager does believe in what is known as reincarnation and Karma. However, if these concepts were exclusively Eastern in origin at one time, then they no longer are for they have been enthusiastically accepted by many in the West. But as a further comment, the New Ager wonders what is wrong with being "Eastern", for in its origin, Christianity was a very "Eastern" religion. And Judaism has absorbed many Eastern elements into its practices. Some of these elements came from Zoroastrianism, some from Mithraism, others from long-forgotten precursors to Judaism. To deny all Eastern elements is to deny a basic part of the Judeo-Christian heritage.

The Apologetics believe that the New Age concept of GOD differs from theirs; but if the Christian concept of God is that which is presented in the Apostles' Creed, then God is the same to both the New Ager and the Christian.

The Apologetics state that the New Ager does not accept JESUS CHRIST as they do, and in some respects, that is true. The New Ager does not believe that Jesus is the only son of God, for there is a considerable amount of language in the Bible which describes Jesus Christ as the son of God uniquely suited to fulfill God's purpose, but not His only son. In this manner, Jesus is to God as Isaac is to Abraham--a special son, but not the only one. In addition, the New Ager feels that he is more nearly a full brother of Jesus than the Apologetics do. With these exceptions, there is little disagreement between the Apologetics and the New Ager in respect to Jesus Christ.

The Apologetics believe that the New Ager does not accept the HOLY SPIRIT in the form of a person of the TRINITY as they do, and they are probably right; but since the Trinity is not biblical, then what justification other than a three hundred year debate is there for accepting it? And the New Ager certainly does believe in a Spirit sent from God.

The Apologetics state that SALVATION as practiced by the New Ager differs from the doctrine of salvation as taught by Christianity and they may be right. Salvation means to be redeemed and thus to be in the presence of the grace of God. It can also mean to be absent from the absence of God. Just as the Apologetics believe that Jesus Christ is the only son of God, they also believe that there is only one way to find God's presence. The mature New

Ager has no problem with the Christian way of finding God; only with its exclusivity.

The New Ager has certain MISCELLANEOUS BELIEFS about the mission of Jesus Christ, the brotherhood of mankind as practiced in the Order of Melchizedek, and the existence of the Office of the Christ. Although these beliefs differ from some orthodox Christian doctrines and dogmas established by man, they were rational and acceptable to those who originally came to God through Jesus Christ; and they should be just as acceptable today to those who come with an open heart.

As a final summary, the Apologetics accept and use as a test for acceptance, certain doctrines and dogmas which the New Ager does not accept. Most of these were established by the church many years after Jesus Christ left this physical plane. Among other dogmas, they include: [1] the exclusivity of Jesus Christ as being the only son of God rather than the son who had a special purpose in God's plan; [2] the concept of the Trinity, which became a non-answer to an unsolvable puzzle; [3] the Christian concept of salvation as being the only workable one; and others. The Apologetics have a sincere belief that their purpose is to defend Christianity against those who attack it or dilute its beliefs. They feel that in doing so, they are serving God's purpose for their lives. There is no question that the mature New Ager respects their beliefs even though he might object to their methods; for although there is no question that many New Agers are Christians in that they choose to follow Jesus Christ and him crucified, the mature New Ager accepts that there may be other ways to the presence of God, and he respects all of them. Furthermore, by proposing the concepts of dimensionality and ascension, the New Ager feels that he is not diluting, but rather enhancing the beliefs of Christianity.

From Toward a World Religion for the New Age
by Lola A. Davis

"The religion which Moses proclaimed and developed on the basis of what he believed were God's commands and revelations, still forms the core of present-day Judaism. But Judaism has changed from the simple, specific and direct statements of Moses to a highly complex, theological system in which many different interpretations are possible. It has been influenced by most of the world's religions and philosophies, as have the other religions. Some of these influences can be seen in the changes of emphasis and content found in the several present-day Judaic groups."

Page 78

"'Who is a Christian?' or 'How do you identify a Christian?' are legitimate questions after reading all the varieties of belief and practice within Christendom. Though some would disagree, I believe the average Christian layman would subscribe to the following description of a Christian:

'A Christian is any person who reveres Christ and tries to follow his teachings as that person understands them'. "

Page 122

206

CHAPTER 8 NEW AGE RELIGION-- DISCONTINUITY OR CONTINUANCE

The Judeo-Christian heritage is a continuance in the sense that Christianity can be considered to be a sequel to Judaism. However, Judaism continues without Christianity. Therefore, although the Judeo-Christian heritage is a continuance, there is also a discontinuity in the sense that Judaism continues as a religion with no input from Christianity. The New Age religion may be a continuance with Christianity, or it may be a discontinuity. To determine which it is, the Judeo-Christian model will be examined to see in what way Judaism-Christianity is a discontinuity and in what way the Judeo-Christian heritage is a continuance. To do this, this Chapter will examine the issue in four sections:

1. How did Judaism-Christianity develop as a discontinuity;
2. How did the Judeo-Christian heritage develop as a continuance;
3. What will happen to Christianity-New Age; and
4. Summary

207

In this Chapter, the term "discontinuity" is defined as "a break, a gap, or a lack of cohesion or continuity"; whereas the term "continuance" is defined as "the act of continuing or a sequel".

JUDAISM-CHRISTIANITY; A DISCONTINUITY

Judaism continues as a religion separate and distinct from the Christian religion. This happened when those of the Hebrew faith did not accept Jesus Christ as the Messiah who had been promised them by their prophets, but only as a teacher similar in character to the many other rabbis or teachers within their faith. To understand why this happened, it is necessary to understand who constituted the Hebrew people at the time that Jesus came to them, and to understand why they chose to reject him as their Messiah.

The Hebrew people were established as a people based on the covenant made by their God with Abraham. In Genesis 12:1-4 it is stated, "Now the Lord said to Abram, 'Go from your country and your kindred and your father's house to the land that I will show you. And I will make of you a great nation, and I will bless you, and make your name great, so that you will be a blessing. I will bless those who bless you, and him who curses you I will curse; and by you all families of the earth will bless themselves' ". Abram went as the Lord had told him. Later, in Genesis 17:5, God said to him, "No longer shall your name be Abram, but your name will be Abraham; for I have made you a father of a multitude of nations." Although the exact dates of these happenings are unknown, most biblical scholars place them at about 2,000 BC.

However, not all of those who were from the seed of Abraham were considered to be Jewish people at the time of Jesus, nor are they so considered today; for Abraham is considered Father Abraham by all Semitic people. Arabs are also Semitic people.

Later, a descendent of Abraham, Joseph, went to Egypt where he was later joined by his kin. Again, the dates are unknown, but it is thought that this happened about 1700 BC. Some 500 years later, the descendents left Egypt. This is known in Jewish history and in the Bible as the Exodus, and is thought to have happened about 1200 BC. During the Exodus, Moses received the next major covenant from God. This was during the time that the Ten Commandments were given to Moses on Mt. Sinai. The covenant was recorded in Exodus 19:5, when God said "Now therefore, if you will obey my voice and keep my covenant, you shall be my own possession among all peoples". However, as will later be developed, not all the people who left Egypt and subsequently conquered the land of Canaan under Joshua were considered to be Hebrews at the time of Jesus, nor are they so considered today.

Later, about 1,000 BC, David became king and united the people. Still later his son, Solomon, built the Temple. After Solomon's death, the nation split into two kingdoms: the northern kingdom of Israel, and the southern kingdom of Judah. The northern kingdom was conquered in about 721 BC and the people were dispersed. In 586 BC [the first date in Hebrew history which is known with certainty], the southern kingdom was conquered and the people were exiled to Babylon. In 538 BC, the Persians conquered Babylon and some of the exiled Jewish people returned to the Jerusalem area under Persian rule.

The only people who were considered to be hereditary Hebrews at the time of Jesus were those who returned from the Babylon exile. This is still true today. These people constitute only a minor fraction of the descendents of Abraham, or of the people who conquered the promised land under Joshua. They are only a minor fraction of the people who had been under David and Solomon. They include none of the tribes who made up the northern kingdom of Israel, and not even all of the people who had been exiled to Babylon. They are solely those who returned from the Babylonian exile.

For some 500 years after the return, the Hebrew people built up a society of their faith while being ruled by others. They were ruled by the Greeks starting in 333 BC and by the Romans in 63 BC. The only time that the land was theirs was for about a 60 year period under the Macabees prior to the Roman occupation. The Romans ruled the land during the time of Jesus; the Persians retook the land in 613 AD; the Arabs followed them in 638; the Turks [Ottomans] came in 1517; and the Turks remained until British rule took over following World War I. Israel was established by a United Nations declaration in 1948. As this history shows, for 2,534 years, God's "chosen people" had no nation of their own. They were held together entirely by their faith.

Because they were never a nation of rulers, but only a nation of faith, their religious faith became very important to their society. It was and still is a faith of the Law and of tradition. At the time of Jesus there was a law to fit almost every possible activity It was a body of law which had been developed during the more than 500 years after the return. As described in Chapter 3, the Pharisees, the largest religious group of Jesus' time, had the job of interpreting the law. They liked their work. Those who rejected Jesus did so in an attempt to retain the Law as they understood it. And why shouldn't they? After all, the Law had been the only thing which had sustained them in their faith for over 500 years.

Jesus Christ proposed that the external law be replaced by an internally generated belief in love and in the brotherhood of man. He said that the great commandment was to love God with all your heart and to love your neighbor as yourself [see Luke 10:27]. During his lifetime, he accepted the Samaritans rather than rejecting them as the Pharisees did; he dined with sinners rather than rejecting them as the Pharisees did; he served his followers by washing their feet rather than having his feet washed as the

Sadducees did; he advocated teaching in the Temple rather than supporting ritualistic worship as the Sadducees did; he advocated working in the Temple rather than ignoring it as the Essenes did; and he advocated paying taxes to Rome [Matthew 22:21] rather than overthrowing Rome as the Zealots wished. As a result, he made every element of the Hebrew society of his day very uncomfortable in his presence. He simply was not the kind of Messiah they had been looking for. Consequently, they rejected him and retained their Judaism. They probably did this for three reasons: [1] they were comfortable with what they had and did not want to be disturbed by something new; [2] they had built up a preponderance of laws, rituals, doctrines and dogmas which generated jobs and which established their way of life; and [3] the Messiah and the new religion which he taught were false because the only true religion was the religion of their fathers.

Judaism survived. It survives today as does Christianity. Although each recognizes that the other exists and there is mutual respect between them, they are separate religions. There is no flow from one to the other. There is Judaism, and there is Christianity. There is a heritage which is shared between them, but there is no continuance. Instead, there is a discontinuity.

JUDEO-CHRISTIAN HERITAGE; A CONTINUANCE

Judaism-Christianity is a discontinuity, primarily because some chose to reject the new belief in Jesus Christ and to remain in the law-driven faith which had sustained them for so many years. However there is a shared heritage between those who were of the Hebrew faith and those who chose to accept Christ as their personal lord and savior. That heritage is commonly called the Judeo-Christian heritage.

In this heritage, Christianity is considered to be a sequel to Judaism. The word "sequel" means "anything that follows; a continuation''. Thus, there is a continuance in the Judeo-Christian heritage. This section will address what caused that continuance to occur.

In explaining himself to his followers, Jesus referred many times to the relationship which he had with his Father. As a few examples, at a very early age he said, ''Did you not know that I must be in my Father's house?'' [Luke 2:49]; and later he said, ''All things have been delivered to me by my Father; and no one knows who the Son is except the Father, or who the Father is except the Son and any one to whom the Son chooses to reveal him.'' [Luke 10:22]; and still later he said, ''I and the Father are one.'' [John 10:30]; and as a final example, he said, ''I am the way, the truth and the life; no one comes to the Father, but by me.'' Obviously, Jesus was claiming a very special relationship with the Father.

And who was this Father? He was the God of the Hebrew nation and people. He was the God who had brought his people out of the land of Egypt. He was the God who said, ''You shall have no other gods before me.'' [Deuteronomy 5:7]. He was the God whose name was pronounced as Jehovah or Yahweh, but whose real name was the Tetragrammaton, the ineffable YHWH.

Because of the way Jesus explained himself to his followers, there became no way that he could be followed without at the same time following the God of the Hebrew people. Consequently, anyone who follows Christ follows him as a sequel to that God. Christianity therefore becomes a sequel to the worship of that God, and for those who accept Christianity, there is a continuance from Judaism to Christianity. It is commonly referred to as the Judeo-Christian heritage.

CHRISTIANITY-NEW AGE; DISCONTINUITY OR CONTINUANCE

It is obvious from sources cited in Chapters 2, 5, and 7 that many of the Christian faith reject everything that is in any way connected to any of the New Age beliefs. They do this in the firm belief that their religion is right and is final. They do this with all of the conviction expressed by the Pharisees and the Sadducees in a similar situation some 2,000 years ago.

It is highly likely that Christianity will continue to function as a religion separate and distinct from the New Age religion just as Judaism has functioned as a religion separate and distinct from Christianity over the past 2,000 years. Thus, there will be a discontinuity. It is highly likely that this discontinuity will be developed for the same reasons that a discontinuity developed between Judaism and Christianity: [1] that those who practice the existing religion feel comfortable with what they have and believe that it is right; [2] that there have been a preponderance of laws, rituals, doctrines and dogmas built up over the years which generate jobs and which establish a way of life which might be disturbed if anything new were to be introduced; and [3] that the new religion is false because the only true religion is the religion of their fathers. Consequently, there will be a discontinuity between Christianity and the New Age.

On the other hand, there are Christians who originally were of the Hebrew faith. In fact, the earliest Christians were of the Hebrew faith, and there would be no Christianity today if some of them had not left their friends and family in order to accept the challenges and beliefs of Christianity, the New Age religion of 2,000 years ago. Later, some of the Hebrew faith wanted to be Christians while keeping all the tenets, creeds, beliefs and dogmas of their Hebrew faith. This was countered by a well-structured dissertation which defined Christ as superior to the angels and to

213

all the Hebrew priests; which defined Melchizedek as superior to Abraham; which defined Christianity as a superior religion to the imperfect religion of Judaism; which stated that to try to hold onto Judaism while being a Christian would dilute the meaning of Christianity; and which suggested that Judaism [which had existed for about 2,000 years] was a prelude to Christianity for which some parts of the world's population were presently ready. That dissertation is known today as "The Letter To The Hebrews" or simply "Hebrews". Those who followed its teaching went on to develop a continuance from Judaism to Christianity which is today known as the Judeo-Christian heritage. They left Judaism by leaving the Temple. Those who neglected the teachings of the book of Hebrews went back to Judaism in the Temple.

Although Christianity could not be practiced without accepting the basis of Judaism which was the belief in one God, today some of the New Age movement are practicing their belief while accepting no input from Christianity. But those who are making the most of their New Age experiences express a belief in Christ every bit as strong as the beliefs which the early Christians expressed in Jehovah. However, they want to participate in the understanding that man's concept of the cosmos has changed greatly since man first interpreted Christ's teachings. These mature New Agers want to accept Christ for all time, but want to accept man's interpretation of Christian teachings as meaningful only in the time in which the interpretation was generated; for they not only believe that man generated much of the interpretative doctrines on Christianity which are accepted as beliefs by the Church today, they also believe that the basis for some of those interpretations and beliefs are not as Christ originally taught. They question why decisions on Christian doctrine which were made 1700 or 700 years ago after much debate and disagreement at the time, should hold the weight of absolute Christian truth today when man's understanding of himself and his environment is so vastly different. They therefore want out of the doctrines, dogmas, fear and control generated by the Church and into the Unconditional Love originally proposed by Jesus Christ and accepted as an Article of Faith by the mature New Ager. In this way, they see a continuance between Christianity and the New Age.

SUMMARY

For reasons which today can be readily analyzed, understood and accepted, some parts of Judaism accepted Christianity and some did not. For the former, there is a continuance between Christianity and Judaism. For them, Christianity has become a sequel to Judaism. For the latter, Judaism exists today as a religion separate and distinct from Christianity. For them there is a discontinuity.

In the same manner, there will be those who remain Christians with absolutely no acceptance of any New Age belief. This will create a discontinuity. In addition, there will be something not experienced in the Judeo-Christian heritage, for there will be those of the New Age who will never have belonged to Christianity or to any other established orthodox religion. They will therefore enter into New Age without a religious foundation from which to grow. This again will represent a discontinuity. But the New Ager who will benefit most from his experiences and who will be the most able to exercise a reasonable acceptance-rejection philosophy, will be the one who has a significant religious background, whatever that background might be. He will therefore be familiar with the restrictive and controlling practices which man has instituted in the name of his religion. As a consequence, he might be able to avoid them. In this way he might permit the faith to make progress restricted solely by the guidelines of Unconditional Love. If that were to happen, then there would be a continuance which would be far superior to that continuance experienced within the Judeo-Christian heritage.

215

And so, at the interface of Judaism and Christianity there was both a discontinuity and a continuance. The same will happen at the interface of Christianity and the New Age religion.

"That life is worth living is the most necessary of assumptions, and, were it not assumed, the most impossible of conclusions."

George Santayana, *The Life of Reason [1905-6], Vol I*

CHAPTER 9   CONCLUSION

Jesus Christ was born in a small town in a small country in a small part of the world. Despite this small beginning, he has arguably had more influence on the affairs of the world that has any other man. His life was short, probably less than 35 years; and his ministry was even shorter, possibly about three years or so. His recorded teachings are not voluminous. They consist of one sermon, some 22 parables, some 7 "I am" sayings, some 18 miracles, and several other examples of how life should be lived. Out of this small packet of teachings, many doctrines, dogmas, and learned dissertations have issued. Out of this small packet of teachings, many "revealed truths" have also issued. By definition, these "revealed truths" are those which must be believed by one who has been baptized, else the one who denies the truth is called a "heretic" or a practicer of "heresy".

As a few examples of activities which were or could have been considered heresy:

1. For the first 300 years of the Christian era, Christianity was decided by Imperial Roman law to be a *religio illicita* [illegal

religion] and all who practiced it were persecuted, sometimes in the most cruel way. To those who did the persecution, the *religio illicita* was probably considered to be a "revealed truth" which must be believed in and obeyed;

2. Because of his victory at the Battle of Milvian Bridge in 312 AD, Constantine became Emperor, embraced Christianity and started to persecute with enthusiasm those who had previously been carrying out Rome's orders to persecute the Christians. Because Constantine became a Christian as the result of a dream, his conversion could easily be considered to be the result of a "revealed truth", even though it was the exact opposite of the "revealed truth" mentioned above;

3. Although there are not many recorded examples of heresy during the first Christian millennium, this may have been because of poor record keeping or because of the lack of "revealed truths". However, in the 12th century things started to pick up. As one example, Arnold of Brescia was excommunicated from the Church because he spoke out against the "revealed truth" [or at least what the Church stated was a revealed truth] that clerics were to live in luxury;

4. In that same century, the Cathari [meaning "pure"] of southern France were declared heretical by the papacy because they spoke out for poverty as contrasted to the luxury of the Catholic hierarchy. They were subjected to a crusade and to the Inquisition. A somewhat similar fate befell the Humiliati of Italy and the Waldenses of northern France;

5. By the 16th century, heresy was becoming quite fashionable. Evidently enough "revealed truths" were now available to ensnare a number of people. One example is William Tyndale who had the heretical idea that everyone should be allowed to read the Bible in his own language. The Church in England prevented him

from translating the Bible into English, so he went to Germany, published the New Testament in English, and was working on the Old Testament when he was captured by the Church, tried for heresy and burned at the stake in 1536;

6. Another example from that century is the heresy of Henry VIII of England who was branded a heretic for declaring that the Church of England was independent of the Church of Rome. Evidently Rome had received a "revealed truth" that the only Church an Englishman could belong to was a Roman Church;

7. Other examples of heresy during that century came from Spain, where the "defense of the Faith" became a reason to torture and execute thousands because they did not profess to believing in the then-accepted "revealed truths";

8. As a final example of heresy in that century, Copernicus [a Cannon of the cathedral in Frauenburg, Poland] developed the theory that the planets revolved around the Sun. He withheld publication for 40 years for fear of being declared a heretic. In the next century, Galileo, inventor of the telescope, was declared a heretic and held under house arrest by the Church for the last eight years of his life for having taught the "false" Copernican theory because everyone "knew" that the Sun revolved around the Earth as a "revealed truth";

9. And of course, there are the heretical activities of Martin Luther [who criticized the Pope], of the English Protestants when a catholic [Mary] was on the throne and of the English Catholics when a protestant [Edward or Elizabeth] was on the throne [because their religion was not that of the throne], and of Jansen [who taught the beliefs of Augustine as contrasted to the beliefs of the Popes];

10. And on and on and on.

Fortunately, in the 20th century, religious toleration has advanced to the point that heresy is starting to fade as a method of defending the Faith. However, today there are still those who believe in inerrancy of their beliefs almost with the enthusiasm of "revealed truths". The purpose of this very short review of the sin of heresy, or denying the "revealed truths" of the Church, is to suggest that the revealed truths which supposedly come from the infallible or inerrant teachings of the Christ whom Christians follow can often be swayed by the political or controlling desires of man. No one has a "lock on truth", for truth is too often a fragile thing, detected solely by the eye of the beholder.

So it is today when each defender of his faith demands from another that "you follow what I say because this is the only true religion." They are suggesting that they have a "revealed truth". In his ministry, Jesus Christ suggested and invited; he did not demand. In his activities, he let his anger out only once when the moneychangers were desecrating the Temple; and in his teachings, he mentioned the place where "men will weep and gnash their teeth" only two times, each of which was in response to inactivity on the part of one of the participants in his parables [the parable of the Talents and the parable of the Wedding Feast]. But other than the righteous anger generated by the Ego-driven misuse of God's sacred house or by the lack of activity which he abhorred, he generated nothing but a sense of love in his activities toward his fellow man, and a sense of gentle persuasion as he taught. And Christ did teach gently, and then when he was finished, he would say, "He who has ears, let him hear." [Matthew 13:9].

We should do likewise, for when talked about in the sense of belief, truth is indeed a delicate subject. In general, each belief will start out with some spark of truth, and then develop itself from there. There are some truths which have been the spark to lead to the beliefs professed by the New Ager. Those truths [T] and beliefs

220

[B] are as follows:

1. The eighty years which we live is a lot shorter than eternity [T], so instead of loafing all the time, maybe the eternal soul of an entity will come back into another body to do some more of God's work [B];

2. A lot of people have left their physical body before us [T], so maybe they are around doing God's work now [B];

3. Since the physical body we presently occupy is so heavy and cumbersome [T], then maybe God has something lighter and easier to use than that with which we are presently encumbered [B];

4. Since this planet is only a very small part of God's universe [T], then maybe He has some interest in other places as well as in Earth [B];

5. Since Jesus Christ was made available to help the people of this Earth [T], then maybe he, or someone like him, has gone to some of the other places and helped the ''people'' there [B];

6. Since the Earth is at most only about a fourth as old as some other parts of the Universe [T], then maybe some of the other parts developed before we did and they are therefore ahead of us, either mentally, physically, emotionally, spiritually, or any combination thereof [B];

7. Since the Earth is over four billion years old [T], then maybe some other parts of the universe are behind our development, either mentally, physically, emotionally, spiritually, or any combination thereof [B];

8. Since we need help [T], then maybe someone who has already trod in the path we are now treading could help us [B];

9. Since others need help [T], then maybe we who have already trod the path they are now treading can help them [B];

10. Since the universe continues to expand [T], then maybe God is continuing to expand also [B];

11. Since eternity is such a long time [T], then maybe we had better start trying to understand what all could go on in an eternity of time and space rather than being quite so concerned about whether or not each person can pass a test which was developed many centuries ago [B]; and

12. On, and on, and on for as long as the mind of man can expand his thinking under the guidance of Spirit.

SUMMARY

Within any movement, whether religious or otherwise, there have been those who have felt that their beliefs represented the only true beliefs. In addition, there have been those who have chosen power or profit over service by letting their Ego drive out their Spirit. The New Age movement has been no exception; and neither has Christianity, Islam, Buddhism, Communism, Capitalism or any other movement. And yet, for those who are Spirit-driven, there is the understanding that no one has an exclusivity on truth; for there is understanding to be found in each of the establishments of belief so long as the goal of the understanding is the goal of Spirit-driven Unconditional Love.

EPILOGUE

Some time in the future, an encounter will occur. The date will probably be some time after the beginning of our year 2001 when the 21st century officially begins; or possibly after the beginning of our year 2012 when, according to the Mayan calendar, the Galactic Synchronization will occur; or possibly after the beginning of our year 2016 when, according to some who communicate with the multi-dimensional ones, some rather unusual events will take place; or possibly even later, for we three-dimensional humans are not evolved enough to overcome the dimension of time and fully understand what the future will hold. But although we do not know when, we do know that the encounter will occur; and we can visualize what it probably will be like.

Although this particular description of that encounter will be presented as if it happened to an allegorical figure, it could happen to any of us, and it probably will. The allegorical figure used in this presentation will be known as Christian.[44] Prior to this encounter, Christian has continued to make Progress through life. He has left Pliant and Obstinate far behind him. Mr. Wordly Wiseman, Vanity Fair and the Valley of Ease have presented no temptation for quite some time; and with good guidance from

223

Knowledge, Experience, Watchful and Sincere, Christian has continued to look forward to his meeting with Hopeful, the final encounter before reaching the wicket gate which opens into Heaven.

As Christian leaves the River of Death and starts up the final hill just before Heaven's Gate, a person appears to him from out of what seems to be nothing other than what we would think were energy waves. After the greetings are exchanged and the small chatter and usual niceties dispensed with, the stranger asks the name of the Pilgrim, and when the answer "Christian" is given, the stranger says, "Oh, does that mean that you are a follower of Jesus the Christ?" When a positive reply is forthcoming, then the stranger says, "He is one of my favorite associates and in fact, I report to him on my activities quite often. I saw him just recently. He was over in the Orion Belt, helping some of the people over there to understand what the purpose of their existence was. He has done that many places, in many worlds and in many forms--even in that oxygen atmosphere of your world which is so terribly poisonous to so many of us. Jesus said he enjoyed his several experiences with you. He seems to enjoy his experience wherever he goes. He enjoys going into many places. He says that in doing so, he is functioning in the many mansions of his Father. He has been very effective."

"Oh my," thought Christian to himself. "How do I handle this?"

Yes, Christian. When the encounter occurs, how will you handle it?

FOOTNOTES AND REFERENCES

1. NOTES FROM THE AUTHOR

2. INTRODUCTION

In the Introduction, as in all other parts of this book unless otherwise stated, the Bible used was the Revised Standard Version published by the American Bible Society, New York and copyrighted in 1980 [Old Testament] and 1973 [New Testament] by the Division of Christian Education of the National Council of the Churches of Christ in the U.S.A. This version of the Bible is constantly being updated for modern English usage by an ecumenical and international council of Protestant and Catholic scholars. It is widely accepted as the standard version of the Bible for English-speaking countries.

In the Introduction, as in all other parts of this book, the Dictionary used for definitions was The American Heritage Dictionary of the English Language published by the American Heritage Publishing Company and Houghton Mifflin Company, New York and copyrighted in 1973. This Dictionary has a distinguished panel which coordinates usage with a distinguished panel of consultants in various specialty fields.

In the Introduction and all throughout the book, the author uses words such as "man" and "he" and "himself" and the like. This is not in any way done to belittle any other sex; but to use "he/her" or "man/woman" or "himself/herself" or the like made the sentence structures so cumbersome as to inhibit communication. The author apologizes for any offense which this may create for some. None is intended.

In the Introduction, and in many other parts of this book, subjects such as "Apologetics", "Pantheism" and the like were researched by using The New Encyclopaedia Britannica, 15th Edition, copyright 1987. When specific notes were taken, then the Britannica has been cited as a footnote.

1. Britannica, Vol. 1, page 486.
2. Britannica, Vol. 16, pages 316-17.

3. PROLOGUE

In addition to the Bible previously mentioned, the Book of Hebrews was researched in several commentaries, including those by Dr. Charles R. Erdman, by J.H. Davies as a part of the Cambridge Bible Commentary series, and by William Barclay as a part of the Daily Bible Study Series.

4. CHAPTER 1 SIMILARITIES AND DIFFERENCES

The references used in this Chapter are presented in the subsequent Chapters which present each subject in greater detail.

5. CHAPTER 2 BELIEF IN GOD

3. Walter Martin, The New Cults [Santa Ana, Cal.: Vision House, 1980] 397

4. John Cornwell, The Hiding Places of God [New York: Warner Books, 1991] 178.

5. John Drane, Introducing the New Testament [San Francisco: Harper & Row, 1986] 113.

6. J.J.Hurtak, The Keys of Enoch [Los Gatos, Cal.: the

Academy for Future Science, 1977] 168.

    7. John F. Walvoord, <u>Major Bible Prophecies</u> [Grand Rapids, Mich.: Zondervan, 1991].

6. CHAPTER 3 JESUS CHRIST, WHO WHERE WHY AND WHAT

    8. Lord Moulton, <u>Atlantic</u>, July, 1924

    9. Drane, 103.

    10. Drane, 99.

    11. Jeffrey Furst, <u>Edgar Cayce's Story of Jesus</u> [New York: Berkley, 1976] 23

7. CHAPTER 4 THE SACRAMENTS

The Britannica supplied most of the reference material for this Chapter.

8. CHAPTER 5 NEW AGE BELIEFS

    12. Dusty Sklar, <u>The Nazis and the Occult</u> [New York: Dorset, 1989] 46.

    13. Sklar, 161.

    14. Sklar, 169.

    15. Taken from the PBS television series <u>Legacy</u>, 1992.

    16. Sklar, 162.

    17. Cornwell, 266-72.

    18. Martin [see Chapter 2 above]

    19. Texe Marrs, <u>Texe Marrs Book of New Age Cults and Religions</u> [Austin, Tex.: Living Truth, 1990].

    20. Billy Graham, <u>Angels: God's Secret Agents</u> [Carmel, N.Y. Guideposts, 1975] 24.

    21. Graham, 19.

9. CHAPTER 6 THE EXPERIENCES OF THE PRESENCE OF GOD

All research on this Chapter is from Britannica, or from personal experiences by the author.

10. CHAPTER 7 CHRISTIAN APOLOGETICS

22. Martin, pages 16-31
23. Martin, page 233
24. a. Helen Wambaugh, Life Before Life [Bantam Books, 1981]
    b. Hans Holzer, Life Beyond Life [Parker publishing Co. West Nyack, N.Y., 1985]
    c. Joe Fisher, The Case for Reincarnation [New York, Bantam Books, 1985]
    d. Marilynn McDirmit, Reincarnation: A Biblical Doctrine? [Eagle Publication Co., Maggie Valley, NC, 1990]
25. Joseph Head and S.L. Cranston, Reincarnation, An East-West Anthology [Theosophical Publishing House, Wheaton, Ill, 1968]
26. The Catholic Encyclopedia, Vol. 11, page 311
27. Head, pages 32-4
28. Head, page 26
29. Head, pages 36-38
30. Robin Westen, Channelers, a New Age Directory [Perigee, New York, 1988] page 20
31. Drane, page 192 quoting Streeter
32. Drane, pages 197 and 461-3
33. The Anchor Bible. The Gospel According to John [Doubleday & Co. Garden City, N.Y., 1966]
34. John Shelby Spong, Rescuing the Bible from Fundamentalism [HarperSanFrancisco, 1991] pages 16 and 214
35. Furst, pages 27 & 28
36. Martin, page 227
37. Spong, page 232
38. Martin, pages 228-30
39. Martin, page 284 et. al.

40. William Barclay, <u>The Letter to the Romans</u>, Revised Edition, The Daily Study Bible Series, [The Westminster Press, Philadelphia, 1975]
    41. Drane, pages 65-68
    42. The Anchor Bible, Volume 36 Hebrews
    43. Hurtak, Glossary

11. CHAPTER 8 NEW AGE RELIGION--DISCONTINU-ITY OR CONTINUANCE

12. CHAPTER 9 CONCLUSION

13. EPILOGUE

    44. All names used in the Epilogue are from <u>The Pilgrim's Progress</u> by John Bunyan

"Then Jesus came from Galilee to the Jordan to John, to be baptized by him. John would have prevented him, saying, 'I need to be baptized by you, and do you come to me?' But Jesus answered him, 'Let it be so now; for thus it is fitting for us to fulfil all righteousness.' Then he consented. And when Jesus was baptized, he went up immediately from the water, and behold, the heavens were opened and he saw the Spirit of God descending like a dove, and alighting on him; and lo, a voice from heaven saying, 'This is my beloved Son with whom I am well pleased.' "

Matthew 3:13-17

APPENDIX--NEW TESTAMENT REFERENCES TO JESUS AS THE SON OF GOD

1. Matt. 3:17 and lo, a voice from heaven, saying "This is my beloved Son, with whom I am well pleased."

2. Matt. 11:27 All things have been delivered to me by my Father; and no one knows the Son except the Father, and no one knows the Father except the Son and any one to whom the Son chooses to reveal him.

3. Matt. 14:33 And those in the boat worshipped him, saying, "Truly you are the Son of God."

4. Matt.16:16 Simon Peter replied, "You are the Christ, the Son of the living God."

5. Matt.17:5 He was still speaking, when lo, a bright cloud overshadowed them, and a voice from the cloud said, "This is my beloved Son with whom I am well pleased; listen to him."

6. Matt. 26:63-4 But Jesus was silent. And the high priest said to him, "I adjure you by the living God, tell us if you are the Christ, the Son of God." And Jesus said to him, "You have said

so...''

7. Matt. 27:43 He trusts in God; let God deliver him now, if he desires him; for he said, ''I am the Son of God.''

8. Matt. 27: 54 ...the centurion...said, ''Truly this was the Son [Note: or a Son] of God!''

9. Mark 1:1 This is the beginning of the gospel of Jesus Christ, the Son of God [Note: other ancient authorities omit the Son of God]

10. Mark 1:11 And a voice came from heaven, ''Thou art my beloved Son; with thee I am well pleased.''

11. Mark 3:11 And whenever the unclean spirits beheld him, they fell down before him and cried out, ''You are the Son of God.''

12. Mark 5:7 and crying out with a loud voice, he said, ''What have you to do with me, Jesus, Son of the Most High God? I adjure you by God, do not torment me.''

13. Mark 9:7 And a cloud overshadowed them, and a voice came out of the cloud, ''This is my beloved Son; listen to him.''

14. Mark 15:39 And when the centurion, who stood facing him, saw that he thus breathed his last, he said, ''Truly this man was the Son [Note: or a son] of God!''

15. Luke 1:31-2 ...and you shall call his name Jesus. He will be great, and will be called the Son of the Most High;

16. Luke 1:35 ...therefore the child to be born will be called holy, the Son of God.

17. Luke 3:22 and the Holy Spirit descended upon him in a bodily form, as a dove, and a voice came from heaven, ''Thou art my beloved Son; with thee I am well pleased.''

18. Luke 4:41 And demons also came out of many, crying, ''You are the Son of God!''

19. Luke 8:28 When he saw Jesus, he cried out and fell down before him, and said with a loud voice, ''What have you to do with me, Jesus, Son of the Most High God? I beseech you, do not torment me.''

20. Luke 9:35 And a voice came out of the cloud, saying,

232

"This is my Son, my Chosen; listen to him!"

21. Luke 10:22 All things have been delivered to me by my Father; and no one knows who the Son is except the Father, or who the Father is except the Son and any one to whom the Son chooses to reveal him."

22. Luke 22:70 And they all said , "Are you the Son of God, then?" And he said to them, "You say that I am."

23. John 1:14 And the Word became flesh and dwelt among us, full of grace and truth; we have beheld his glory, glory as of the only Son from the Father.

24. John 1:18 No one has ever seen God; the only Son, who is in the bosom of the Father, he has made him known.

25. John 1:34 And I have seen and have borne witness that this is the Son of God.

26. John 1:49 Nathanael answered him, "Rabbi, you are the Son of God! You are the King of Israel!"

27. John 3:16-18 For God so loved the world that he gave his only Son, that whoever believes in him should not perish but have everlasting life. For God sent the Son into the world, not to condemn the world, but that the world might be saved through him.

28. John 5:25 Truly, truly I say to you, the hour is coming, and now is, when the dead will hear the voice of the Son of God, and those who hear will live.

29. John 6:69 and we have believed, and have come to know, that you are the Holy One of God.

30. John 10:36 do you say to him whom the Father consecrated and sent into the world, "You are blaspheming" because I said "I am the Son of God"?

31. John 11:4 But when Jesus heard it he said, "This illness is not unto death; it is for the glory of God, so that the Son of God may be glorified by means of it."

32. John 11:27 She said to him, "yes, Lord; I believe that you are the Christ, the Son of God, he who is coming into the world."

33. John 17:1 When Jesus had spoken these words, he lifted

up his eyes to heaven and said, "Father, the hour has come; glorify the Son that the Son may glorify thee

34. John 19:7 The Jews answered him, "We have a law, and by that law he ought to die, because he has made himself the Son of God."

35. John 20:31 but these are written that you may believe that Jesus is the Christ, the Son of God, and that believing you may have life in his name.

36. Acts 9:20 And in the synagogues immediately he proclaimed Jesus, saying "He is the Son of God."

37. Rom. 1:3-4 the gospel concerning his Son, who was descended from David according to the flesh and designated Son of God in power according to the Spirit of holiness by his resurrection from the dead, Jesus Christ our Lord,

38. Rom. 1:9 For God is my witness, whom I serve with my spirit in the gospel of his Son, that without ceasing I mention you always in my prayers,

39. Rom 8:32 He who did not spare his own Son but gave him up for us all, will he not also give us all things with him?

40. II Corin. 1:19 For the Son of God, Jesus Christ whom we preached among you

41. Gal. 2:20 I have been crucified with Christ; it is no longer I who live, but Christ who lives in me; and the life I now live in the flesh I live by faith in the Son of God, who loved me and gave himself for me.

42. Gal. 4:4-7 But when the time had fully come, God sent forth his Son, born of woman, born under the law, so that we might receive adoption as sons. And because you are sons, God has sent the Spirit of his Son into our hearts, crying, "Abba! Father!" So through God, you are no longer a slave but a son, and if a son then an heir.

43. Eph. 4:13 until we all attain to the unity of the faith and of the knowledge of the Son of God, to mature manhood, to the measure of the stature of the fulness of Christ;

44. Heb. 3:6 but Christ was faithful over God's house as

a son.

45. Heb. 4:14 Since we have a great high priest who has passed through the heavens, Jesus, the Son of God, let us hold fast our confession.

46. Heb. 5:5 So also Christ did not exalt himself to be made a high priest, but was appointed by him who said to him, ''Thou art my Son, today I have begotten thee''

47. Heb. 5:8 Although he was a Son, he learned obedience through what he suffered;

48. Heb. 7:1-3 For this Melchizedek, king of Salem, priest of the Most High God, met Abraham returning from the slaughter of the kings and blessed him; and to him Abraham apportioned a tenth part of everything. He is first, by translation of his name, king of righteousness, and then he is also king of Salem, that is, king of peace. He is without father or mother or genealogy, and has neither beginning of days nor end of life, but resembling the Son of God he continues a priest forever.

49. II Peter 1:17 For when he received honor and glory from God the Father and the voice was borne to him by the Majestic Glory, ''This is my beloved Son with whom I am well pleased.''

50. I John 1:3 ...our fellowship is with the Father and with his Son Jesus Christ.

51. I John 1:7 ...and the blood of Jesus his Son cleanses us from all sin.

52. I John 2:22-24 Who is the liar but he who denies that Jesus is the Christ? This is the antichrist, he who denies the Father and the Son. No one who denies the Son has the Father. He who confesses the Son has the Father also. Let what you heard from the beginning abide in you. If what you heard from the beginning abides in you, then you will abide in the Son and in the Father.

53. I John 3:8 The reason the Son of God appeared was to destroy the works of the devil.

54. I John 3:23 And this was his commandment, that we should believe in the name of his Son Jesus Christ and love one another, just as he commanded us.

55. I John 4:9-10 In this the love of God was made manifest among us, that God sent his only Son into the world, so that we might live through him. In this is love, not that we loved God but that he loved us and sent his Son to be the expiation for our sins.

56. I John 4:14-5 And we have seen and testify that the Father has sent his Son as the Savior of the world. Whoever confesses that Jesus if the Son of God, God abides in him and he in God.

57. I John 5:5 Who is it that overcomes the world but he who believes that Jesus is the Son of God?

58. I John 5:9-12 If we receive the testimony of men, the testimony of God is greater; for this is the testimony of God that he has borne witness to his Son. He who believes in the Son of God has the testimony in himself. He who does not believe God has made him a liar, because he has not believed in the testimony that God has borne to his Son. And this is the testimony, that God gave us eternal life, and this life is in the Son. He who has the Son has life; he who has not the Son of God has not life.

59. I John 5:20 And we know that the Son of God has come and has given us understanding, to know him who is true;

CHAPTER 10   ADDENDUM

After this book had been completed and set in type for printing, some additional information became available which cleared up two points that had been bothering the author. The information was received only recently, in January, 1993, and consequently was too late to be included in the text of the book. It is therefore offered for consideration in this Addendum. The information was generated by one on Earth who can communicate with the multi-dimensional ones. Such people are commonly called "channelers".

As mentioned earlier in this book [see pages 124-5], one of the basic beliefs of the New Age is that there are beings of consciousness which exist in dimensions not discernible by the five physical senses of humanity. However, just as Billy Graham believes that angels talk [see page 125], many of the New Age believe that some Earth-bound humans can become a vehicle through which the multi-dimensional ones can talk. In this manner, the messages are transmitted in a way that they can be heard by the human physical senses because the Earth-bound human has become a "channel" for communication.

It is not the purpose of this book to justify channeling or to subscribe to its authenticity in any way; for just as there are Christian preachers or teachers who talk one way while acting another, there are channelers who let their own ego interfere with anything which might otherwise come through as a message of understanding. Consequently, whereas most of this book could be considered as *intellectual theology* in that it has been carefully researched and documented with information generally recognized as being valid, this Chapter should be considered in the realm of *speculative theology* in which the author is merely presenting some channel-developed information for speculation or consideration. In this, as in all cases with channeled information, the recipient should always apply an acceptance-rejection analysis similar to that proposed on page 17; for if any recipient accepts everything that has been presented without determining how it fits within its own spirit-guided soul or ''self'', there is a chance that he could become ego-led or controlled.

Within these parameters, this Chapter will present information on two puzzles. One of these puzzles has bothered many Christians; the other has bothered many of the New Age. The first of these puzzles relates to the interaction between Jesus and the money-changers in the temple; and the second relates to the existence of the ''twin flame''. Since this information was received through the efforts of a ''channeler'', it should be considered to be ''speculative theology'' and received solely in that spirit.

A CHRISTIAN PUZZLE   As mentioned on page 18, Jesus introduced a new order of things--**love** instead of **law**. In view of this, many Christians who have read the scriptures have been confused as to why Jesus did such an uncharacteristic thing as to use physical force against the money-changers in the Temple; for as recorded in John 2:13-16, ''The Passover of the Jews was at hand, and Jesus went up to Jerusalem. In the temple he found those who were selling oxen and sheep and pigeons, and the money-changers at their business. And making a whip of cords, he drove them all, with sheep and oxen, out of the temple; and he poured out the coins of the money-changers and overturned their tables. And he told those who sold the pigeons, 'Take these things away; you shall not make my Father's house a house of trade.' "

Have you ever wondered why Jesus, a divine being who had the power to calm the winds and the sea [Matthew 8:26], would resort to the use of a common, physical force such as the whip to calm down common men? Why could he not have used a more divine power to serve that purpose?

During a message channeled in early January, the following understanding was presented:
"But at the time that the Master Jesus came, man had become so invested in flesh and ego that there was scarcely enough spiritual light upon the Earth to support that the Christed one could live here. The whole angelic host came together to empower the energy that he could even be birthed into the flesh safely. And therefore he accepted a great challenge and had a tremendous test imposed upon him at all times; for he had to be very careful to stay clear of emotional involvement. That is why he never took a woman; because that would have taken emotional energy which he could not give up. That is also why he never beat the money-changers, for that also would have required a tremendous emotional involvement. But then, why should he beat them? Why would a Master who could calm the waves have to take a whip against his brothers? Those who reported on this stood on the outside and assumed many things. He did go into the temple, and he did feel much righteous indignation there; but as a Master, he called forth an image unto each one of those who were there and spoke to them at their soul level. He said to them, 'You will meet what you most fear'; and then the illusion of their own terror appeared before their own inner eyes. One person would not have seen what another person would have seen, for each one saw that

of which he was most afraid. They overturned their own tables and beat themselves out of the Temple. But in their chaos and confusion, they swore that the Master did it; for his thought was like a lash upon their soul. In reality, it was their own guilt which had abused them.''

Although this is only speculative theology, it does give comfort to think that Jesus may have followed his teachings of love rather than participate in physical abuse, even of the money-changers who had desecrated the temple. Instead of physically abusing them, he made them understand their own shortcomings, and with that understanding, they abused themselves.

Although this understanding could represent an solution to this Christian puzzle, the author is not presenting this thought as anything other than a possibility. It is something which should be considered by those who believe that the Christ walked on Earth with a constant feeling of love. To have anyone see themselves as they are could be an act of love; whereas to physically abuse them would not be an act of love such as he constantly preached. As it says in Matthew 13:9, ''He who has ears, let him hear.''

A NEW AGE PUZZLE As mentioned on page 116 of this book, some New Agers believe that their soul has split into a male part and a female part in order to gain experiences; and that one goal of their existence is to find their other half, or ''twin flame''. On the other hand, other New Agers believe that the soul has not split, but that the male and female exist as one androgyny within self. Many New Agers are confused as to why there is such a dichotomy within the New Age belief system.

In one part of the channeled message, the following information was presented:
''For some, the *twin flame* does exist, but it would be rare that it would come into the Earth plane at the same time as the other

part of itself; for one part of the soul exists in the etheric while the other part journeys in flesh. If the two parts do not fully mature at the same time, then neither part can ascend. And so, while one is moving toward the realization of ascendancy here, the other is balancing from the other side. However, a *twin soul*, or one who vibrates with much of the same harmonic frequency, can exist with another twin soul on this plane. There is more than one twin soul, but there is only one twin flame. Twin souls exist all over the universe, but the twin flame will exist only when the original generation of the soul occurred on a planet of duality. This would then require a splitting of the soul into duality and would generate the existence of a twin flame. On planets which have never split into duality, each soul would generate itself as being complete within self. Planets that have promoted duality or separation have done so by the belief that God is out there and man is here, and that man and woman are separate but can not live without each other. But it is meant that each one would learn to love both the man and the woman within itself; for if woman does not appreciate the man that she is, then she will not exist well with her brothers, and if a man does not honor the woman that he is, then he surely will not honor his sisters.

"But even though some souls will not have a twin flame, all souls will have twin souls, some of which will be incarnate at the same time and others which will not. Perhaps there would be as many as a hundred twin souls, not necessarily all of them in flesh at the same time. There are also *soul mates*. There are many soul mates, both male and female, with whom you have made an agreement at a soul level to complete something. You may not always feel too kindly about them or even like them, for you have come to settle an old issue or to give a gift. After this is done, then you may split asunder and go your different directions. Twin souls and soul mates are different; for a soul mate is not necessarily one whom you love; whereas a twin soul is. However, you also must love yourself very well to be with a twin soul for they will mirror everything.

"And so, there is only one *twin flame*, there are several [say, a hundred] *twin souls* and there are many many *soul mates*. And yet there are so many who journey as if they were completely alone. They wonder if there are any others like them on this planet. Of course there are! There are not so many; for where the eagles fly, there are not vast numbers. But if you grant yourself permission to be truly loved, then you will find that there are many who love you, whether they are a twin flame, a twin soul or just a soul mate with whom you have some uncompleted task to finish."

Again, as mentioned on page 116, there is a dichotomy within the New Age. There are many who have questioned the existence of a twin flame. For those who wish to accept the understanding presented above, the absence of a twin flame is now understandable; for it is believed that these entities have come from an original source which did not exist in duality, but in androgyny. There are also many who have ardently believed in and searched for their twin flame. This also can now be understood; for it is believed that these entities have come from an original source which did not exist in androgyny, but in duality. This difference in original source explains why some have felt the existence of and need for the twin flame; whereas others have not. This understanding is offered solely as a thought which might be able to overcome some confusion.

CONCLUSION   For those who would permit their soul to evaluate the messages received through channeling, some puzzles can be solved by developing an understanding which is not available through any other emotional or intellectual source. The "truth" of this understanding can only be judged by the eye or the ear of the beholder as guided by spirit working through his soul-- for only this kind of judgment can permit the final evidence or evaluation of any truth.

ACKNOWLEDGMENTS

I offer thanks to the Ascended Masters who helped me to put this book together; and to the various Christian Sunday School classes who indicated to me what teachings they would accept and what teachings were not meant for their present acceptance. They did this by their interest or their lack of same. I also thank my wife, Jan, and my daughter, Sherry, for their encouragement, suggestions and proofreading skills.

Excerpts from *The Nazis and the Occult* by D. Sklar, copyright ©1977 by Dusty Sklar and reprinted with his kind permission.

Excerpts from *Angels, God's Secret Agents* by Dr. Billy Graham, copyright © 1975 by Billy Graham. Reprinted by permission of Word, Inc., Dallas, Texas.

Excerpts from *Rescuing the Bible from Fundamentalism* by John Shelby Spong, copyright © 1991 by John Shelby Spong. Reprinted by permission of HarperCollins Publishers.

Excerpts from *The Anchor Bible* reprinted by permission of Doubleday and Company, Inc.

Excerpts from *The Daily Bible Series* reprinted by permission of The Westminster Press.

Cover Illustration by Sheryl Moore

ORDER INFORMATION

For additional copies of this book, please send orders pre-paid to:

PENDULUM PLUS
3232 COBB PARKWAY
SUITE 414
ATLANTA, GA 30339

Price for a single book is $12.95 plus $1.05 for shipping and handling to total $14.00

To encourage group study and discussion, the price for a package of five books sent to a single address is $39.00. This price includes postage and handling within the United States.

To further encourage group study, the price for a package of 20 books sent to a single address is $140.00 This price includes postage and handling within the United States and will also include a short, pertinent teacher's manual for group study which also may by used for individual study Other copies of the study manual are available for $1.00 each if ordered with a book or books.

For Georgia residents, the state tax of 5% is to be added to the prices mentioned above.

Telephone orders will not be accepted. However, dealers or distributors may request a large volume discount schedule by calling Dave or Jan Moore at: **404-435-6355**